FOR-PROFIT COLLEGES AND UNIVERSITIES

FOR-PROFIT COLLEGES

AND UNIVERSITIES

Their Markets, Regulation, Performance,
and Place in Higher Education

Edited by
*Guilbert C. Hentschke, Vicente M. Lechuga,
and William G. Tierney*

Foreword by
Marc Tucker

STERLING, VIRGINIA

COPYRIGHT © 2010 BY
STYLUS PUBLISHING, LLC.

Published by Stylus Publishing, LLC
22883 Quicksilver Drive
Sterling, Virginia 20166-2102

Library of Congress Cataloging-in-Publication-Data

For-profit colleges and universities : their markets, regulation, performance, and place in higher education / edited by Guilbert C. Hentschke, Vicente M. Lechuga, and William G. Tierney ; foreword by Marc Tucker. — 1st ed.
     p. cm.
     Includes index.
     ISBN 978-1-57922-424-0 (cloth : alk. paper) — ISBN 978-1-57922-425-7 (pbk. : alk. paper)
     1. For-profit universities and colleges—United States. 2. Education, Higher—Economic aspects—United States. I. Hentschke, Guilbert C. II. Lechuga, Vicente M. III. Tierney, William G.
     LB2328.52.U6F67 2010
     378'.04—dc22   2009032275

13-digit ISBN: 978-1-57922-424-0 (cloth)
13-digit ISBN: 978-1-57922-425-7(paper)

Printed in the United States of America

All first editions printed on acid free paper
that meets the American National Standards Institute
Z39-48 Standard.

Bulk Purchases

Quantity discounts are available for use in workshops
and for staff development.
Call 1-800-232-0223

First Edition, 2010

10   9   8   7   6   5   4   3   2   1

To Peg, Debbie, and Barry, who were able to figure out what to do without us while we wrote the book and took us back once we finished it.

CONTENTS

FOREWORD

Many years ago, when I was an undergraduate at Brown University in the 1950s, I noticed that a couple of my friends were different, very different, from everyone else. Pierce and Randy were returning veterans of the Korean War. They were a little older than the rest of us. But that did not by itself account for the difference.

These two young men knew why they were in college. They were a lot less interested than I was in trying to understand my place in the cosmos, and much more interested in acquiring the skills and knowledge they would need to get a good job and build the network of friends and acquaintances that would enable them and their families to do well in a rapidly changing society and economy. They didn't join fraternities. They didn't drink themselves silly on Saturday night, or any other night. They studied hard and did well and kept their eye on the ball. But real wages have actually been declining for years now, and jobs-for-life now appear to be jobs-until-bankruptcy. Nothing seems secure, and, increasingly, the best job insurance seems to be more and better education and skills training and everyone knows it.

What they want is meat and potatoes. What they are interested in is getting the skills and knowledge they need to compete in a world that is getting more competitive by the minute. And they want this at the best possible price they can get it for, no frills.

Marc Tucker
President & Chief Executive Officer,
National Center on Education and the Economy, and
Co-Chairman,
New Commission on the Skills of the American Workforce

I

FOR-PROFIT COLLEGES AND UNIVERSITIES IN A KNOWLEDGE ECONOMY

Guilbert C. Hentschke, Vicente M. Lechuga, and William G. Tierney

U ntil recently, for most of us, *higher education* immediately called to mind familiar postsecondary institutions such as community colleges (mostly public), liberal arts colleges (mostly private), state colleges (public), and research universities (public and private). Within the last generation, a new type of institution has grown up and firmly planted itself among these familiar *higher education* categories: the for-profit college and university (FPCU). Educating over two million students each year (JBL Associates, Inc., 2007), FPCUs have reached the consciousness of students and others through extensive marketing campaigns and the now-familiar freeway signs directing drivers to nearby campuses.

Increasing proportions of society are recognizing a causal connection between increased postsecondary schooling, increased employability, increased income, and increased quality of life—a connection that motivates individuals to pursue more schooling. The benefits accrue to them directly and indirectly, not only as members of households but also as employees and citizens. Partly in response to this demand, providers of postsecondary schooling—both existing and aspiring—are responding, or at least trying to respond. In contrast to public and private nonprofit entities, for-profit enterprises, characteristically, might be expected to respond to a business opportunity. This has been the case in the higher education sector. Much of this response has been from private for-profit enterprises, which, by definition, "do" education or schooling but also "behave" like businesses. They use the language of colleges and universities but operate like corporations or sole proprietorships.

As private businesses that prepare students for specific occupational roles, FPCUs are not new as a type. Foster's Commercial School of Boston, considered to be the first established proprietary school to specialize in training for commerce, was founded by Benjamin Franklin Foster in 1832 (Imagine America Foundation, 2008). Noted historically for providing relatively short programs in several dozen occupational fields leading to certificates and diplomas, FPCUs now provide certificate and degree programs in over two hundred occupational fields ranging from art to business to information technologies and education to health sciences and culinary arts. The rise of FPCUs to prominence, however, is relatively recent, from less than 1% of all students attending higher education in the early 1970s to 9% in 2006–2007 (JBL Associates, Inc., 2007), or about one-half of the current market share of private, nonprofit traditional colleges and universities (TCUs). Much of this growth can be attributed to their focus on providing postsecondary options to nontraditional student populations, a constituency that has, until recently, been all but ignored by TCUs. Nontraditional students have not only been underserved, but also represent a major growth path in higher education. FPCUs have focused directly on these students but are now a major concern of educators in our compulsory system, in our traditional higher education institutions, and in our workforce development communities.

Size and Scope of FPCUs

FPCUs are, on average, small. They constitute 39% of all institutions in higher education, but only about 9% of its enrollments. Most FPCUs (about 1,380) offer programs that are less than two years long, followed by those that offer two-year programs (about 850), and then those that offer four-year programs (about 450) (Gubins, 2007). Through their industry-specific, career-specific, and even job-specific focus, FPCUs now award 15% of all associate's degrees in higher education, 4% of all bachelor's degrees, 8% of all master's degrees, and 3% of all doctoral degrees in American higher education (see Table 1.1). FPCUs offer *career-oriented* programs for which there are there are proportionately large numbers of workplace vacancies. The most popular

TABLE 1.1
Share of Total Degrees Awarded by Institutional Type, 2005–2006

Institutional Type	Associate's Degrees (%)	Bachelor's Degrees (%)	Master's Degrees (%)	Doctoral Degrees (%)	Professional Degrees (%)
Public	78	64	49	60	41
Private Nonprofit	7	32	43	37	58
For-Profit	15	4	8	3	1

Source: *The Chronicle of Higher Education,* Chronicle Almanac, 2007–2008.

associate's degree programs are in health professions and related clinical services; business, management, marketing; and computer and information sciences. The most popular *bachelor's* degree programs include the aforementioned categories as well as visual and performing arts, and security and protective services.

FPCUs offer programs leading to *certificates* as well as degrees. In fact, as a group, FPCUs award more certificates than degrees (about 60% to 40%). When enrollments in both certificate and degree programs are added together, the focus on large, high-demand career fields is even more evident. Health professions are far and away the most popular, plus widely diverse occupational fields such as mechanic and repair technologies; engineering technologies; education; legal professions and studies; transportation and materials moving; and construction trades (Imagine America Foundation, 2008). Individual FPCUs usually focus on a relatively narrow subset of career specialties. Compared to TCUs, each FPCU offers few "majors" and even fewer electives.

The *current* size of the higher education market occupied by FPCUs is the result of the recent, disproportionate growth of FPCUs (see Figure 1.1). Fall enrollments at *institutions* with programs lasting four years or more increased most rapidly in the for-profit sector, 52% between fall 2003 and fall 2006 (National Center for Education Statistics [NCES], 2005–2006, 2006–2007). Enrollments in *programs* lasting four years or longer increased 25% at FPCUs between 2003 and 2006 (NCES, 2005–2006, 2006–2007). The number of degree-granting FPCUs grew 22% between 2000 and 2005. Even the number of *non*–degree-granting FPCUs increased by 3% during that time (NCES, 2005–2006, 2006–2007).

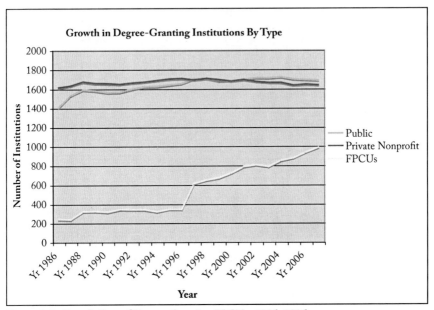

Figure 1.1 Growth Rate of Degree-Granting FPCUs, 1986–2006
Source: U.S. Department of Education, *Digest of Education Statistics, 2007.*

FPCUs as Businesses

FPCUs have clearly arrived, but their "place" within the field of higher education is still to be affirmed. FPCUs are awkwardly situated within the public policy framework of higher education. Postsecondary education, historically provided largely by nonprofit and public organizations and considered a public good, is now also being provided by for-profit businesses, demonstrably providing significant private as well as public benefits, a trend that raises two interrelated questions that are explored more deeply in Chapter 8: What *public* support and oversight should be provided to FPCUs that is different from that which is provided to any other for-profit consumer services industry? Should the form of public support and oversight be any different from that provided to all other postsecondary education institutions? Said differently, what would be the justifications for providing or not providing public support to FPCUs? The answers to these questions are more complex than they may initially appear. FPCUs are tax-paying, job-generating, investment-attracting businesses that serve to raise workforce educational levels—all attributes highly prized by most national, state, and local governments. At the same time, FPCUs can be viewed as recently arrived, profit-seeking interlopers on the student markets of traditional colleges and universities whose relations with governmental bodies are of long standing.

The unsettled nature of their position in higher education today comes from a combination of issues that have arisen along with the rise of FPCUs. Chief among these issues is the for-profit status of these enterprises: Should an organization be permitted to function *both* as a classic "institution of higher education," enjoying the public support of its mission and operation, and at the same time be able to operate as a private profit-seeking business pursuing financial returns for its investors? This business vs. education tension within FPCUs manifests itself in institutional priorities, in the work of its faculty (Chapter 3), and in how FPCUs are regulated (Chapter 5) and accredited (Chapter 7).

A Framework for Examining FPCUs as Businesses

FPCUs are often evaluated and described from a single, widely accepted *business* framework that emphasizes financial performance, rates of growth, and prospects for future profitability—a framework fundamentally different from those applied to the TCUs. As for-profit entities, FPCUs have different constraints and rights, and they face different incentives than do TCUs. The right of individuals to trade (i.e., buy and sell) shares of FPCUs makes FPCUs a potential vehicle for profit-seeking investors. Indeed, their capacity and propensity for raising investment capital, both through equity and debt, *explains* their disproportionate growth in higher education. While all institutions seek at some level to earn at least as much, if not more, in revenues than is incurred in expenses, FPCUs are additionally *profit*-seeking organizations. The fundamental means by which they seek profit is through a combination of increases in scale (volume) and in margins (between costs and revenues). Investors, for their part, pursue revenues though their decisions to invest in and withdraw investments from FPCUs.

FPCUs pursue these incentives within the constraints and opportunities characteristic of for-profit enterprises. Tuition at FPCUs is generally higher than at most public TCUs, but less than the average tuition charged by private TCUs. In contrast to TCUs, all FPCUs pay taxes—over $80 million in 2005 (JBL Associates, 2007). Generally they receive no direct financial support from state governments, unlike public two- and four-year institutions that receive state and federal appropriations. FPCUs pursue and receive virtually no gifts or donations, and they do not create endowments. They do, however, benefit indirectly from government subsidies, largely in the form of federal student financial aid that allows students to choose among eligible colleges.

The Role of Federal Financial Aid

FPCU eligibility for federal student aid is determined in part by accreditation status. By virtue of acquiring accreditation, most FPCUs participate in Title IV federal student aid programs (e.g. Pell grants, Stafford loans), just as most TCUs do. Students attending degree-granting FPCUs are more likely than their TCU counterparts to apply for federal aid (98%), to receive Pell grants (72%), and to receive Stafford loans (91%). (Goan & Cunningham, 2007). As of 2005, the 2,694 Title IV FPCUs constituted 39% of all Title IV postsecondary institutions in the country, and serve about 2.1 million students annually (JBL Associates, 2007). A very large proportion of FPCU revenue, then, comes from tuition, and a very large proportion of tuition is subsidized either through grants or loans to students.

Unlike most TCUs, FPCUs are not guaranteed existence, and certainly not financial success. Like other businesses, they can fail and go away. As is the case with other investment options, investors assume risks when investing in FPCUs. Financially related characteristics that pose potential problems to FPCUs include "execution risks" (poorly performing management), regulatory risks, increased payment delinquency, and increased competition. Most of the factors that contribute to the relative success or failure of a FPCU can be linked to its financial metrics, especially those measuring its recent performance history. This is more the case for FPCUs than for TCUs. To stay in business and attract additional sales and investment, FPCUs have to perform well enough financially. This is not to suggest that issues of financial health are not as central to TCUs, but it does suggest what constitutes "success" for TCUs is less overtly financial on its face.

Performance Characteristics

By virtue of the fact that FPCUs are for-profit institutions, they are most frequently evaluated through a relatively homogeneous *financial* template that focuses analysis on the organization's financial health (see Chapters 2, 7, and 8). A wide variety of standard accounting measures are routinely employed in most analyses of FPCUs, collectively providing information on three broad business dimensions of an FPCU: its performance as a business, the quality of its earnings, and its valuation (Debenham, Schiffman, Allworthy, & Evans, 2005). Measures of *business performance* reflect in differing ways the effectiveness of management, and include measures that have meaning only for those schooled in financial analysis, such as return on capital employed, return on equity, operating margins, earnings per share growth, and free cash flow. Differing measures of the *quality of earnings* test the underlying security of business performance and include asset replacement ratio, tax rate, and net debt–equity ratio. Measures of *valuation* connect in differing ways the economic performance of the FPCU to its market value, and include price–earnings ratio, dividend yield, and free cash flow yield. While "performance" and "valuation" have meaning among TCUs, most of these aforementioned financial measures do not—but they are important constructs for understanding for-profit enterprises. (Cf. Debenham, Schiffman, Allworthy, & Evans, 2005.) While designed for consumption by multiple audiences, these frameworks are designed primarily to provide information to senior management and present and future investors for use in evaluating the investment value of the business.

Dozens of such measures, routinely applied to individual FPCUs, provide both a common framework to evaluate FPCUs' financial health in a manner common to other businesses—but unlike nonprofit and public colleges and universities. While TCUs routinely supply annual reports containing summary balance sheets (financial status at a point in time) and income statements (financial activities over a certain period), financially constructed frameworks associated with performance of for-profit enterprises are largely absent. (One exception to this generalization in TCUs is the scrutiny applied to endowment performance for those TCUs that have them.)

Various performance characteristics are revealed by, inferred from, or associated with these financially related data: the degree to which the FPCU is pursuing a fast-growing market, the degree to which its programs align with relevant segments of the market, the degree to which profitable program specializations and courses can be easily replicated across campuses in other labor markets, and the degree to which the FPCU has strong brand recognition (it is widely recognized as having attractive characteristics).

Financial and educational priorities do not always align with each other. Consider, for example, the issues associated with nontraditional student markets. On the one hand, these students have constituted an extensive untapped market (a desirable business feature). On the other hand, the characteristics of many of these students (low levels of prior academic achievement, low income, low wealth, independent status or having dependents, etc.) suggests that they present greater completion and credit risks than do traditional students (an undesirable business feature) (Gubins, 2008). Either way, FPCUs are joining with TCUs to serve them—but they are not alone.

Other "Schooling Businesses" in Higher Education

Increased demand for schooling has fostered the growth of FPCUs and, to a lesser extent, TCUs, but these are not the only types of firms responding to increased demand for more highly skilled employees. Although the focus of our work here is FPCUs, we do not want to convey the impressions that postsecondary education is now composed *solely* of FPCUs and TCUs, that they compete *only* with each other, and that the two kinds of institutions constitute the sum and total of higher education's universe. Other types of schools are also emerging (see Cantor, 2000; Garrett, 2005; Hanna, 1998). The other types do not look exactly like either TCUs or FPCUs, but—like TCUs and FPCUs—they also provide schooling services to adults.

Stated another way, FPCUs are only one form of higher education outside the traditional academy (Cantor, 2000). One of these other forms can be described more as "training and human resource development" delivered by *non-education* firms for employees and customers. In the field of information technology, corporate vendors and professional associations have created well over 300 discrete certifications since the first such credential (Certified Novell Engineer or CNE) was issued in 1989 (Adelman, 2000). By early 2000, about 1.6 million individuals worldwide had earned 2.4 million information technology certifications.

Corporate Universities

In addition to the FPCU, another form of postsecondary "school" has emerged. Corporate universities are often located within large, often multinational corporations, although they sometimes partner with TCUs.

Corporate universities grew out of the corporate human resources departments, which have taken on increasing responsibility for treating their firms' workforce more as an asset ("human capital") than an expense item ("cost of labor"). Corporate universities also grew in recognition of the value of certification of the training provided for employees by employers. Their original student focus was their own employees, but some have since opened up their schools to non-employees. These entities now number in the thousands (Allen, 2002; Meister, 1998), and their names often reveal their corporate parentage—Dell University, Disney Institute, FORDSTAR, General Motors University, Oracle University, Sears University, and Xerox Management Institute.

Online Learning

A third type of "school" entails low- or no-cost study-via-the-Internet programs developed by TCUs as well as FPCUs. They address specific subjects and are prepared explicitly for students to pursue but do not necessarily charge any tuition or provide for any examination of achievement or certification of course completion. More than "free content on the Internet," these initiatives develop and provide online courses free of charge. Individuals can join networks of users to both take and develop courses. Carnegie Mellon's Open Learning Initiative is but one example (see Carnegie Mellon University, 2008; Thille, 2008). TCUs and FPCUs develop applications of Web-based technology and apply them to courses in engineering, chemistry, and biology, which represents an educational form that differs from online instructional programs, whose business model requires user payment.

Nonprofit Organizations

Fourth, a growing number of nonprofit community-based organizations (e.g., Corporation for Public Broadcasting, American Red Cross) are providing free and fee-based education and training in a wide variety of subjects not only for children, but for adults "in competition with traditional institutions of higher education" (Cantor, 2000, p. 1). As an example, Annenberg Media urges teachers: "Start school with FREE professional development and K–5 teacher resources from Annenberg Media, including *Arts in Every Classroom, Essential Science for Teachers, Teaching Reading,* and *The Whole Child*" (Annenberg

Media Learning Organization, 2008). Free programming is provided in arts, foreign languages, literature, mathematics, science, and social studies for four categories of students: K–4, 5–8, 9–12, and college/adult.

Certificates and Diplomas

Fifth, a separate group of for-profit, *nondegree* providers receives education services from or provides services to TCUs "but also undertake activities judged to directly or indirectly compete with [TCUs]" (Garrett, 2005, p. 18). Although too diverse to briefly summarize, these firms include for-profit college networks that lack degree-awarding powers (e.g., AEC Education, Singapore; INTI Universal Holdings, Singapore), software/IT training firms (e.g., Aptech, India; Informatics Holdings, Singapore), student support specialists (e.g., IBT Education, Australia; DMGT, UK), and multinational publishers or content providers (Pearson, UK; Thompson, Canada). Garrett includes in this group FPCUs that do not award degrees (only certificates and diplomas) and excludes those that do.

While including a much wider range of postsecondary education businesses than would be included in our limited definition of FPCU, this brief list reveals many firms that find themselves close to inclusion. Not unlike corporate universities and technical training programs inside IT firms, there are many new types of providers in the adult schooling business in addition to FPCUs. Some of them compete with each other and with TCUs and FPCUs; others provide complementary services to each other; still others function somewhat like FPCUs. With relatively minor alterations—e.g., formal admission, certification of satisfactory completion, accreditation—some could become FPCUs.

From this perspective, the increases in postsecondary schooling are much more pervasive, multiformed, and expansive than have been captured in our categorical analysis of FPCUs and TCUs. Developments in postsecondary schooling are outpacing our ability to track them consistently, coherently, and comprehensively. The demands of a knowledge economy are manifesting themselves in a proliferation of new forms of schooling providers. Nonetheless, FPCUs and TCUs together still constitute a very, very large share of the postsecondary schooling universe, and it is within this context of increasing demand for schooling coupled with new kinds of schooling providers that FPCUs have emerged.

Growth in the Knowledge Economy

After decades of rapid growth and steadily increasing market share, FPCUs are at a new point in their history—but so are TCUs. *All* are growing (albeit at quite different rates) within the context of an emerging "knowledge economy." One of the historic justifications for public support of higher education was its contribution to the public good (see Chapter 8)—referring in part to the benefits that others accrue when an individual is educated. That historic perspective has, if anything, taken on greater meaning today, and governments at all levels do what they can to promote workforce development, in part due to the presumption of broadly shared benefits. Strangely, FPCUs are relatively unconnected to these public "workforce development" efforts, perhaps due to their relatively recent arrival as collectively large-scale providers of job training.

FPCUs, Public Initiatives, and Workforce Preparation

Federal, state, and regional governments have historically supported a wide variety of efforts to improve the education levels of the workforce within their jurisdictions, including tracking data on jobs, providing subsidies for job training, overseeing regional economic development initiatives, and creating and staffing commissions on workforce readiness. The U.S. Department of Labor, for example, tracks job demand and predicts a significant increase from now through 2016 in occupations that require postsecondary training. Jobs requiring an associate's degree are projected to be in most demand, with a projected increase of 19% (Bureau of Labor Statistics [BLS], 2003). FPCUs focus their efforts on training for sizeable occupations that face high growth, such as nursing, information systems, business, and several health-related fields identified by governmental agencies such as the BLS. However, their involvement in workforce preparation initiatives is limited at best.

State and regional workforce development initiatives, unlike those at the federal level, heavily involve some providers of career-related schooling, and yet FPCUs appear not to be included in any substantial way. This is odd, especially given the low completion rates of students with multiple "completion risk factors"—i.e., those that TCUs have had difficulty serving. FPCUs provide the labor market with a relatively high share of people of color compared to TCUs. In 2005–2006, over 280,000 minority graduates from

FPCUs were able to enter the labor market, compared to 569,460 minority graduates from TCUs and 36, 916 from historically black colleges and universities (NCES, 2005–2006, 2006–2007). Students at two-year FPCUs have a higher completion rate (38%) than students at public community colleges (17%) (NCES, 2003–2004).

Policies to engage postsecondary education institutions in state economic development vary widely across the states and include an equally wide variety of actors, such as governor's and legislative offices, departments of higher education, K–12 education, economic development and commerce, private business sector representatives, nongovernmental organizations devoted to community and economic development, and faculty and labor councils (Zaleski, 2007). FPCUs, individually or in association, are largely missing from these deliberations.

Zaleski's (2007) review of public policies on workforce development suggested that states are investing in three workforce development mechanisms: (1) collaborative research, (2) workforce development programs, and (3) economic development boards, commissions, and councils. These mechanisms have not adequately addressed some employers' concerns. As illustrated in the work of California's Postsecondary Education Commission, employers are not only concerned with specific occupation shortages (e.g., teaching, nursing, engineering), but also worry that many career-oriented programs do not provide graduates with "twenty-first century skills" such as problem solving, critical thinking, and the ability to work in teams (California Postsecondary Education Commission [CPEC], 2007). These frustrations have prompted many employers to hedge their bets on various "commissions," opting instead "to work directly with postsecondary institutions within their region to build a shared understanding of regional economic needs and identify the types of education and training programs needed to better prepare students for jobs in current and emerging sectors" (CPEC, 2007, p. 4), much like FPCUs do with local employer advisory boards.

FPCU noninvolvement in workforce development policy circles may be due to the inherent separateness of the postsecondary education and workforce development establishments. FPCUs represent a unique confluence between two worlds that are not extensively integrated—postsecondary education and workforce development. As FPCUs seek to straddle both of these worlds, they are fully integrated in neither. One illustration of this is reflected in the programmatic organization of the National Governors Association, where workforce development programs are separate from postsecondary education programs (National Governors Association, 2008).

The lack of connection between workforce policy development and individual FPCUs in California extends beyond the lack of formal FPCU involvement in workforce policy development. Recently, California's Bureau for Private Postsecondary and Vocational Education—the public body responsible for oversight of the 1,000+ FPCUs and their 400,000+ students in the state—closed its doors, at least temporarily (CPEC, 2007). This has left the California Postsecondary Education Commission and the California workforce policy community in general effectively cut off from FPCUs. While in the future, CPEC "may elect to . . . offer options on how [FPCUs] may best contribute to California's workforce development efforts . . . [i]t is not possible to do more than acknowledge their existence at this time" (CPEC, 2007). Through their production of career-prepared graduates and their working relationships with area employers, FPCUs have a significant impact on workforce development. Their voice in state-level workforce development policy, however, appears not to be as significant.

As governments face globalization pressures and seek to attract and grow more educated workforces, they will be confronted with a variety of new private postsecondary education providers that are quite different from those found in the familiar Carnegie Classification System of TCUs. This growing variety of postsecondary schooling options (programs, pathways, majors, and providers) are generally workplace- and career-related—like FPCUs. This particular supply of schooling options raises questions about the degree to which students are seeking out them out. What do students want from a college experience these days? It is difficult to imagine these newer kinds of schooling options lasting very long if students did not inherently value what the institutions were providing. Pursuing higher education entails a significant expenditure of time and money (even if subsidized), so that student perspectives on higher education ultimately influence what programs will grow and which ones will not. Like higher education providers, student attitudes toward higher education are also changing.

Changing Student Attitudes Toward College-Going

Some form of ongoing communication between regional FPCUs, TCUs, and workforce policy actors will likely become more in evidence as competitive workplace pressures mount, and also as changing student attitudes toward college-going increasingly favor economic benefits. Increasing proportions of students are coming to believe and value the old saying: "The more you learn, the more you earn." They would now probably add "more and more." There is a growing sense among students that the link between education and income is of more importance today than in the recent past (Astin, 1998). This could explain the growth of FPCUs, although its unique effect is difficult to measure. Per annual research on the attitudes of entering college freshmen:

> Agreement with the statement that "the chief benefit of a college education is to increase one's earning power" increased from 53.6% to 70.9% between 1969 and 1989. Similarly, the percentage of students who say they were attending college "to be able to make more money" increased from 49.9% to 74.7% between 1971 and 1991. (Astin, 1998, p. 121)

This shift is not a temporary reaction spurred by a downturn in the business cycle. Rather it signals a more fundamental, long-run rethinking of the value of higher education. Every year since 1966, the opinions of nearly 10 million college freshman have been recorded across more than 1,500 accredited colleges and universities (Astin, 1998), and the shift appears to be permanent.

> [S]ome of the most pronounced changes during the past 30 years are in students' values. Especially notable are the changes in the importance given to two contrasting values: "developing a meaningful philosophy of life" and "being very well off financially. . . . In the late 1960s, developing a meaningful philosophy of life was the top value, endorsed as an "essential" or "very important" goal by more than 80% of the entering freshmen. "Being very well-off financially," on the other hand, lagged far behind, ranking fifth or sixth on the list with less than 45% of the freshmen endorsing it as a very important or essential goal in life. Since that time, these two values have basically traded places, *with being very well-off financially now the top value* (at 74.1% endorsement) and developing a meaningful philosophy of life now occupying sixth place at only 42.1% endorsement. (Astin, 1998, p. 124)

This shift in students' perceived value of a postsecondary education began in the early 1970s, continued until the late 1980s, and has remained in its current position ever since.

Rapid enrollment increases in FPCUs also *may be* largely attributable to their extensive marketing techniques. At the same time, it seems equally plausible that changes in student motivations like those described by Astin may be contributing to a greater valuing of the employment prospects derived from college experiences. The financial dimensions of FPCUs are relevant not only to investors and managers, but also to students. *Their* motivation for investing time and money in FPCUs is driven in large part by the economic returns that come from successful program completion implied by job placement (or promotion) within a focused occupational category. The average rate of return on a career college education is 31.25%, well above any interest rate a student would receive had they invested their money instead of going to college (JBL Associates, Inc., 2007).

Overview of the Book

The dynamic, commercial, and "unsettled" nature of FPCUs is conveyed throughout the subsequent chapters of the book. We focus, in the broad sense, on three interconnected areas regarding for-profit higher education—marketplace influences, policy considerations, and issues pertaining to the public good—with emphasis on their interconnectedness. Markets both shape and are shaped by government policies and rules of the game; assumptions about the public good and the role of government shape policies and regulations, which, in turn, affect both the demand for and the supply of postsecondary education services. This chapter, along with Chapters 2 and 3, considers the influence of the marketplace on courses and programs, faculty work, nontraditional student enrollment, and the overall growth of the for-profit higher education sector, while Chapters 5, 6, and 7 explore various policy considerations that affect FPCUs, including federal regulation and oversight, accountability and assessment, and legal and regulatory issues FPCUs face internationally. Finally, issues pertaining to the public good are explored in Chapters 4 and 8, specifically those addressing the notion of academic freedom and the distribution of public monies to FPCUs. Regardless of the topics addressed here, FPCUs are more developing than they are fully developed. In their examination of individual dimensions of FPCUs, the authors have sought to convey both the current state and the unresolved issues facing these businesses. In so doing, they have surfaced enduring topics that face all of postsecondary education.

In "Evolving Markets of For-Profit Higher Education" (Chapter 2), Guilbert Hentschke examines the interplay of two features that have shaped for-profit higher education over the last three decades—the characteristics of students enrolled and their numbers. During that period FPCUs have grown very rapidly, largely by offering career-programming to non-traditional students, including students that were not aggressively sought by TCUs. Hentschke tracks this recent history and then uses it to examine how FPCUs are evolving, especially with regard to the newer programs they currently provide and the additional students they are enrolling. In particular, he examines five extensions of the nontraditional student market that FPCUs appear to be pursuing, all in response to the growing private and public value of workforce skills.

FPCUs are now an integral part of higher education; they provide the training and skill sets most sought after by employers. Nevertheless, FPCUs are still in business to make a profit and the way in which FPCUs utilize faculty plays an integral role in profit generation. "Who Are They? And What Do They Really Do?" (Chapter 3) examines faculty work at one FPCU as a means of exploring the broader issues that faculty members who work at FPCUs face when academics and profits collide. More specifically, Vicente Lechuga explores the influence of the market on particular aspects of faculty work, including participation in curriculum design, governance, and other related activities at one corporately owned and publicly traded for-profit institution. Through a series of in-depth interviews with part-time and full-time faculty, this case study explores the nature of faculty work to understand how external forces affect the roles and responsibilities of faculty and how profit generation impacts faculty work life at FPCUs.

Academic freedom remains a fundamental tenet of academia that frames faculty work at traditional nonprofit colleges and universities. In "Differences in Academic Work at Traditional and For-Profit Postsecondary Institutions: Policy Implications for Academic Freedom" (Chapter 4), William Tierney and Vicente Lechuga contrast the academic work lives of faculty members at public and private nonprofit institutions with those at for-profit institutions as a pretext for a larger discussion on academic freedom. The authors argue that academic freedom at FPCUs is of peripheral concern because it is not an essential element that defines how faculty work is structured at these institutions. Of consequence, the characteristics that frame faculty work at FPCUs place them in a fundamentally different stance with regard to serving the public than those that frame faculty work at TCUs. The authors conclude that a major challenge relates to whether postsecondary institutions are able to clearly define policies that enable faculty at both traditional and for-profit institutions to perform to the best of their ability.

The way in which higher education in the United States is structured places the onus on individual states to create and implement policies that govern how colleges and universities operate and are organized. Nevertheless, federal regulation and oversight remains a necessary component of our higher education system, as do policies related to the distribution of federal financial aid monies.

In "Markets, Regulation, and Performance in Higher Education" (Chapter 5), Mark Pelesh provides readers with a detailed examination of higher education regulation and oversight and how federal policy situates FPCUs within the higher education realm. Pelesh focuses on the interplay between accrediting bodies, state, and federal regulatory systems and how this "triad of regulation" impacts the role FPCUs play. He argues that the emerging market in which higher education is situated necessitates action by FPCUs to engage in the legislative and regulatory processes with regard to higher education policy.

Assessment and accountability are two of the most pressing issues in higher education today, and FPCUs lead the way in answering these calls. In "Accreditation and Accountability: The Role of For-Profit Education and National Accrediting Agencies" (Chapter 6), Elise Scanlon and Michale McComis lay out a detailed history of the largest national FPCU accrediting body (the Accrediting Commission of Career Schools and Colleges of Technology, or ACCSCT), revealing in the process its evolution of function— from association to accrediting body to accountability monitor. Since 1998, the ACCSCT requires its institutions to provide accountability measures to the organization, such as program completion and job placement rates, before they can be accredited. By 2002, the ACCSCT assessment model had been institutionalized across the country. The authors argue that given the attention paid to quantitative and qualitative assessment measures, FPCUs and national accrediting bodies are in an advantageous position when it comes to setting national accountability standards for all of higher education.

The literature on for-profit higher education is dominated by discussions of FPCU behavior within the United States. However, not only does for-profit ownership exist in other countries, but the growth of the private sector globally parallels the recent expansion of U.S. for-profits (Kinser & Levy, 2006). In addition, economic globalization and the provision of cross-border education services have significant implications for the for-profit sector, making it important to address its international dimensions. In "A Global Perspective on For-Profit Higher Education" (Chapter 7), Kevin Kinser draws upon data gathered through the Program for Research on Private Higher Education, an international collaboration of scholars devoted to understanding the recent development of private higher education. He sketches the scope of for-profit higher education outside the United States, characterizes the various legal and regulatory models that apply to the provision of education at a profit in international contexts, and describes the role of for-profit entities in the global business of education.

The ubiquitous nature of private businesses in postsecondary education raises a most fundamental issue of their public good, an historic attribute of traditional colleges and universities. In "The Public Good in a Changing Economy" (Chapter 8), William Tierney first traces the idea of the public good as it has been conceived in general—and, with regard to education, in particular. He then critiques what this suggests for for-profit education and how traditional definitions of the public good fit, and do not fit, the needs of the United States in the twenty-first century. In order to highlight his argument, Tierney utilizes data on students who attend traditional postsecondary institutions and for-profits and compares their completion rates. Tierney argues that a sense of, and a commitment to, the public good is essential for a democratic society, but that how the public good gets played out in society may change over time.

Closing Thoughts

Higher education outside the United States is gaining ground on U.S. higher education. Within the last few decades, "the U.S. share of the global college-educated workforce has fallen from 30% to 14%, notwithstanding a very large increase during the same period in the fraction of Americans entering college" (National Center on Education and the Economy, 2007, p. 16). Increasing growth and increasing vulnerability are simultaneous, a notable phenomenon given the very large size of higher education relative to the entire education industry. Spending on higher education makes up nearly 2.3% of U.S. GDP (Silber, 2006) and about 40% of all spending in the education industry, which totaled $1.04 trillion in 2006—making education among the three largest sectors of the GDP (Silber, 2006). These three to four thousand institutions with which we are so familiar are structured and governed, virtually without exception, as public or private *nonprofit* organizations. These same institutions face an uncertain collective future. In the increasingly "flat world," other nations are catching up in higher education, just as they have in other fields, At the same time, U.S. higher education is evolving—in part toward programs with more explicit career relevance.

To the historic private nonprofit and public institutions are now added nearly 3,000 *for-profit* education businesses with growing prominence and a focused mission on career preparation, generating jobs and tax revenues. Moreover, the nontraditional student populations to which FPCUs cater not only have been underserved, but also represent a major growth path in higher education. On one hand, and in a historical sense, FPCUs are a recent arrival on the higher education scene—growing but not fully accepted, and still fundamentally evolving. On the other hand, and from a public policy perspective, FPCUs occupy the "center" of U.S. education in today's knowledge economy. How so? FPCUs sit at the intersection of three "adjacent" education establishments that provide students with various postsecondary education options: compulsory schooling, higher education, and workforce preparation. FPCUs functionally interact with all three. We suggest here added engagement between these establishments. Greater "vertical" as well as "horizontal" articulation among these sectors could significantly benefit today's students—both traditional, but especially nontraditional—who must negotiate today's higher education bazaar of options. Those benefits extend beyond the private and personal to include the public and societal. Our modest goal in this text is to situate FPCUs at the intersection of three postsecondary establishments by focusing on the subsequent chapters on three distinct areas—marketplace influences, policy considerations, and issues of public good. In our view, the potential of the role FPCUs will play within the higher education bazaar has yet to be realized.

References

Adelman, C. (2000). *A parallel postsecondary universe: The certification system in information technology.* Washington, DC: U.S. Department of Education, Office of Educational Research and Improvement.

Allen, M. (Ed.). (2002). *The corporate university handbook: Designing, managing, and growing a successful program.* New York: AMACOM.

Annenberg Media Learning Organization. (2008). *Teacher resources and teacher professional development programming across the curriculum.* Retrieved August 2, 2008, from www.learner.org.

Astin, A. W. (1998). The changing American college student: Thirty-year trends, 1966–1996. *The Review of Higher Education, 21*(2), 115–135.

Bureau of Labor Statistics. (2003). *Tomorrow's jobs 2006 and projected 2016: Occupational outlook handbook.* Washington, DC: U.S. Department of Labor.

California Postsecondary Education Commission. (2007). *How California's postsecondary education systems address workforce development* (Report No. 07-21). Sacramento, CA: Author.

Cantor, J. (2000). Higher education outside of the academy. *ASHE-ERIC Higher Education Reports, 27*(7), 1–84.

Carnegie Mellon University. (2008). Open learning initiative: OLI courses improve learning outcomes. Retrieved August 28, 2008, from www.cmu.edu/oli/.

The Chronicle of Higher Education. (2008). *The* Chronicle *almanac, 2007–2008.* Washington, DC: Author.

Debenham, K., Schiffman, M., Allworthy, B., & Evans, D. (2005). iQmethod: Our approach to global equity valuation, accounting, and quality of earnings. New York: Merrill Lynch Global Securities Research & Economics Group.

Garrett, R. (November 2005). The Global Education Index: 2005, Part 2: Public Companies—relationships with non-profit higher education. London, The Observatory on borderless higher education.

Goan, S. K., & Cunningham, A. F. (2007). *Differential characteristics of 2-year postsecondary institutions.* Washington, DC: National Center for Education Statistics, U.S. Department of Education.

Gubins, S. (2007, September 10). Signs of stabilization: Increasing student funding. *Education and Training Services Bi-Weekly: Industry Overview.* New York: Merrill Lynch.

Gubins, S. (2008, March 10). Education conference highlights: Focus on lending. *Education and Training Services Bi-Weekly: Industry Overview.* New York: Merrill Lynch.

Hanna, D. E. (1998). Higher education in an era of digital competition: Emerging organizational models. *Journal of Asynchronous Learning, 2*(1), 66–95.

Imagine America Foundation. (2008). *Career college history.* Retrieved September 1, 2008, from www.imagine-america.org.

JBL Associates, Inc. (2007). *Economic impact of America's career colleges.* Washington, DC: Imagine America Foundation.

Kinser, K., & Levy, D. C. (2006). For-profit higher education: U.S. tendencies, international echoes. In J. Forest & P. Altbach (Eds.), *The international handbook of higher education*. Dordrecht, the Netherlands, and London, UK: Springer Publishers.

Meister, J. C. (1998). *Corporate universities: Lessons in building a world-class work force*. New York: McGraw-Hill, Inc.

National Center for Education Statistics. (2005–2006, 2006–2007). *Enrollment survey, 12-month unduplicated headcount: Academic years 2005–06, 2006–07, DAS*. Washington, DC: U.S. Department of Education.

National Center for Education Statistics. (2003-04). *Beginning postsecondary students longitudinal study: First follow-up (BPS: 04/06), DAS*. Washington, DC: U.S. Department of Education.

National Center on Education and the Economy. (2007). *Tough Choices or Tough Times. The Report of the New Commission on the Skills of the American Workforce*. Hoboken, NJ: Jossey-Bass.

National Governors Association. (2008). NGA center for best practices, our divisions. Retrieved August 28, 2008, from www.nga.org/portal/site/nga.

Silber, Jeff M. (2006). "Equity research: Education and training." New York: BMO Capital Markets, U.S. (February).

Thille, C. (2008). *Evidence based design: The open learning initiative*. Retrieved August 28, 2008, from http://edcommunity.apple.com/ali/print.php?itemID=11365.

Zaleski, A. (2007). *Policies to engage postsecondary education in state economic development*. Denver: Education Commission of the States.

2

EVOLVING MARKETS OF FOR-PROFIT HIGHER EDUCATION

Guilbert C. Hentschke

O ver the course of only a few decades, for-profit colleges and universities have emerged as a recognized, distinct sector of U.S. higher education alongside other more traditional postsecondary sectors such as community colleges (largely public), liberal arts colleges (largely private, nonprofit), and research universities (public and private, nonprofit). Their rise to greater visibility is attributable to a combination of features, including their private for-profit status, collective career focus, pursuit of "nontraditional" or "marginal" students, and rapid growth, which significantly exceeds that of traditional colleges and universities (TCUs). Extraordinary enrollment growth of these nontraditional students at FPCUs is the focus of this chapter. (The other features mentioned are examined in the following chapters.)

The early stages of this upsurge, roughly three to four decades ago, were accomplished through the pursuit of students that traditional institutions were not aggressively recruiting. These students did not have backgrounds or aptitudes that historically aligned with pursuit of a college degree, and traditional institutions did not actively seek them out due to a combination of capacity constraints and a ready pool of students with sufficient college-going capabilities and interests. Over subsequent decades, FPCUs significantly increased their market share of students enrolled in all of higher education to roughly 8–9%, up from 2–3% over that period. More precise figures depend on the institutional criteria used to include FPCUs and TCUs (accredited or not) and in the programs the students attended (certificates and/or degrees).

What does past growth suggest for future growth? Are FPCUs pursing students with even more nontraditional characteristics? Or, rather, are FPCUs seeking to move "up-market"? Will their historical career emphasis evolve? If so, is it toward the programs that more nearly resemble TCUs, or toward even greater career emphasis?

The first half of this chapter examines the extent to which FPCUs have pursued marginal students and, in the process, captured a larger share of the entire higher education market in the United States. In the second half, we look at five ways that FPCUs are extending their historic pursuit of marginal students and moving further into old territories as well as into new.

Pursuing Growth in Areas of Low (or Non-existent) Competition

FPCUs are outgrowing TCUs. Their disproportionate growth is due in large part to their disproportionate *pursuit of growth.* FPCUs are responding to incentives inherent in for-profit enterprises, behaving like profit-seeking businesses do in all other industries. They seek profitability by developing a suite of distinctive, consumer-valued products and services, and their growth is a fundamental manifestation of their success. FPCUs have grown rapidly from a small base of about 0.4% of all degrees granted in 1974 to 4% of all degrees granted in 2000 to about 6% of all degrees granted in 2006 (Silber, 2006). Current estimates (discussed later in this chapter) place their market share at around 8%. TCU enrollments have not shrunk; they are growing much more slowly than FPCUs.

Since 2003–2004, enrollments at FPCUs have increased by 17%, and nearly half of all students attending a for-profit during 2005–2006 were enrolled at institutions that offered bachelor's, master's, or doctoral degrees (JBL Associates & Wilson, 2007). They have grown in enrollments partly as a result of their collective focus on workforce preparation, and despite their relatively high price in comparison to public TCUs.

FPCU enrollment growth is simultaneously flowing toward higher degrees and certificates of greater program length or duration. In other words, their offerings are gradually beginning to mirror those of TCUs. In terms of growth, FPCUs are outpacing TCUs in enrollments, in the number of institutions, and in the number of degrees granted. TCUs graduate the vast majority of students, but FPCU graduates are growing at a much faster rate. There are also differences in growth rates within the ranks of FPCUs, with publicly traded, larger FPCUs growing faster than privately held, smaller ones. FPCUs that specialize in longer, more degree-directed programs are growing faster than those with shorter, certificated-directed programs. FPCUs with programs that utilize distance delivery are growing faster than those that do not.

Growth Incentives

The characterizations mentioned above do not adequately describe how the profit-seeking motivation of FPCUs influences their pursuit of growth, nor do they sufficiently explain how different motivations of TCUs induce them to pursue other measures of success. Profits derive from the interaction of margins (roughly the difference between unit production costs and sales revenue) and scale (number of units sold). If for only this reason, FPCUs place a higher priority on enrollment growth (and scale) than do TCUs. Each behaves differently with respect to student admissions and institutional capacity. TCUs seek to maximize student quality (measured variously), subject to capacity constraints. They will admit the most qualified students possible, subject to limits on their capacity. The least qualified students at a TCU are those that the TCU "just barely had room for." FPCUs, on the other hand, seek to maximize capacity (enrollments), subject to quality constraints (measured variously) (Tierney and Hentschke, 2007). Rather than letting capacity determine the lower bound of the quality pool, as TCUs do, FPCUs set that lower bound and then enroll as many students as they can, and will grow their capacity in order to enroll more students if there seems to be more students than current capacity can accommodate.

This does not suggest that all TCUs are prestigious any more than it suggests that all FPCUs experience enrollment growth. (Some TCUs do not have the drawing power to fill their entering class, and some FPCUs have closed their doors after losing enrollments.) It *does* suggest, however, the *pursuit* of different ends—"growth" at FPCUs vs. "prestige" at TCUs (Brewer, Gates, & Goldman, 2002). This difference is, of course, subject to enormous variation among TCUs and FPCUs. Some TCUs are pursuing growth strategies, and some FPCUs are creating programs to attract students at higher degree levels. But, in general, TCUs and FPCUs differ in the degree to which each embodies elements of a traditional school and a traditional business, such as profit-maximizing growth vs. capacity-constrained prestige maximization, growth in enrollments vs. growth in residual demand (i.e., ratios of applications to admissions, admissions to acceptances, and acceptances to enrollments), career focus vs. broad liberal education, and nontraditional vs. traditional student markets.

Size and Growth

When it comes to growth, size appears to matter for FPCUs. All else being equal, larger FPCUs tend to grow at higher rates than smaller FPCUs. The most visible and widely recognized—and fastest-growing—FPCUs are those relatively large, often publicly traded multistate, multicampus systems offering career-oriented degree and nondegree programs—often referred to as "super systems"—like Apollo, Career Education Corporation, and the U.S. Education Corporation (Silber, 2006). Several factors account for this, like economies of scale in operation and marketing that can take advantage of geographically diffuse locations. Large, *multicampus* FPCUs can "roll out" newly designed programs to students and employers to several different regional markets. An information technology program at Career Education Corporation, for example, could be implemented across its 78 campuses in different parts of the country; Corinthian Colleges could do the same with one of its health professions programs across its 90 campuses, as could Kaplan, Inc., with one of its business programs across its 102 campuses (JBL Associates, 2008).

Not all FPCUs are growing—or can grow—as rapidly as these. About half of all FPCUs are smaller, single- or few-campus businesses usually operating solely within a region. They, too, have a career-oriented focus and rely heavily on relations with local employers to assess and respond to market shifts, but as a group they are not growing as quickly (Silber, 2006). One example of an enterprise college is Ohio Valley College of Technology (OVCT), a one-campus FPCU located in East Liverpool, Ohio. Founded in 1886, OVCT currently provides programs in accounting, computers, dental and medical assisting, and health information programs (JBL Associates, 2008).

The third and relatively newest of the FPCU business models, "Internet institutions," operate predominantly via virtual classrooms and have no physical campuses, in contrast to institutions whose Internet offerings complement offerings on their campuses. Examples include Capella and Jones

International University (Silber, 2006). These are growing about as rapidly as the very large FPCUs, but from a much smaller base.

Marginal Students

As alluded to earlier, FPCUs did not grow their share of the higher education marketplace by initially competing with TCUs. Rather, they pursued students who were collectively *less* in evidence at TCUs, more at the margins than the center of TCU target markets. These include disproportionate numbers of students who are independent or who have no parental support, have incomes in the lowest quartile, have parents with an education below the high school level, and are racial or ethnic minorities (JBL Associates, 2008). In 2005–2006, 37% of students enrolled in FPCUs were minorities, compared with 25% in public TCUs and 20% in private, nonprofit TCUs (JBL Associates & Wilson, 2007). More recent data puts the number of FPCU students who are minorities at 43% (JBL Associates, 2008).

FPCUs graduate disproportionately high percentages of minority students, as contrasted to their 8% share of *all* higher education students enrolled. Of degrees conferred at FPCUs, 38% went to minorities, compared to 19% of those at public and 16% of those at private, nonprofit TCUs (JBL Associates, 2008). Of those who received an associate's degree, 22% of all African-Americans and 19% of all Hispanics earned it at a career college (JBL Associates, 2008). Among all who earned certificates in higher education, nearly two-thirds of Hispanic students and about half of all African-American students got them at FPCUs. FPCUs currently account for about one-fifth of all associate's degrees earned in the United States by African-American and Hispanic students (JBL Associates, 2008). In 2003, nearly 61% of Hispanics attending two-year FPCUs graduated, whereas at the same time 44% and 18% of Hispanics graduated from two-year nonprofit, and public TCUs respectively (JBL Associates, 2008).

Many minority students at FPCUs are, coincidentally, from low-income households. Among all two-year higher education degree-granting institutions, FPCUs enrolled the highest proportion (37%) of dependent students with family incomes of less than $25,000 (Goan & Cunningham, 2007).

Bachelor's and graduate degree attainment by minorities is more anecdotal, but in the same direction of overrepresentation at FPCUs. Six of the top ten institutions producing minority graduates with bachelor's degrees in computer and information science were FPCUs, with DeVry Institute being at the top. Moreover, of the top ten institutions awarding master of business administration degrees to minorities, four were FPCUs, according to Borden, Brown & Majesky-Pullmann (2007). These disproportionate numbers are explained, in part, by the relatively narrow program focus of individual FPCUs: DeVry's bachelor's degree program in computer and information science represents a very large fraction of its total enrollment, which is not the case with TCUs that have the same program.

Will FPCUs continue to focus on nontraditional students—and, if so, will future cohorts be any more or less college-ready than past cohorts? Past FPCU student cohorts had more nontraditional characteristics than present cohorts. As recently as 2003, only 75% of FPCU students had earned a high school diploma, and 29% were single parents. Over half were in the lowest income quartile, and the parents of nearly two-thirds of FPCU students had a high school education or less (JBL Associates, 2003). Does this suggest a trend line of movement *away from* nontraditional, even marginal students? Perhaps, but not necessarily.

Penetrating markets by serving "marginal students." The way that FPCUs have entered and grown in higher education is not too dissimilar from the way that other new firms with innovative goods and services have penetrated other well-established industries or fields. Indeed, some have argued that this is how many, if not most, major innovations happen in any industry (Christensen, 2007). Firms with a new business model enter an existing field—not by competing against well-established firms for their customers, but by "competing against non-competition" (Christensen, 2007; Christensen & Raynor, 2003; Christensen, Horn, & Johnson, 2008). With FPCUs, this has meant providing services for those students least pursued by traditional colleges and universities—students who are older, who have smaller incomes, who are not as academically prepared, who come from racial and ethnic minority backgrounds, who are self-supporting (no parental support), and who already have children and, possibly, full-time jobs.

Disruptive innovations are not major breakthroughs that arrive with great fanfare and visibility. Nor are they immediately heralded as "innovations." Rather, the argument goes, they often entail modest beginnings, with entrepreneurs creating new products and services using a different, often less costly, business proposition, and selling them to people with few other options. Initially, those products or services are not as good as those offered to current markets by established competitors. For FPCUs, "inferior" usually connoted things like no dorms or athletic programs, few library resources, fewer full-time (and virtually no tenured) faculty, and campuses in office parks and shopping malls. Those "inferior" services can succeed in the marketplace only because the new firms are not directly competing for the same customers as traditional providers of that service. Rather, they attract customers that have no or very few other choices, and for whom the "stripped down" model of higher education is better than no higher education. Going forward, how do FPCUs continue to serve these and other student markets?

Beyond Nontraditional Students: Extending FPCUs' Historic Student Market

With growing demand for postsecondary schooling and a host of new kinds of schooling providers, not to mention new TCU program initiatives, FPCUs' pursuit of growth is shaped in part by its past success in continuing to do what it has always done. As discussed in Chapter 1, FPCU is a delimiting category—"only those private, for-profit businesses that are almost entirely in the business of postsecondary education, but with the limited focus on largely accredited, certificate- and degree-based career preparation programs in a pre-specified set of occupational fields." Although limiting to a degree, FPCUs still represent a wide variety of individual business distinctions—distinctions that begin to reveal forces, circumstances, and ultimately, strategies of individual firms.

FPCUs have moved relatively aggressively to provide services for nontraditional students, and in so doing have relied on a growing variety of strategies, tactics, and organizational forms. "Nontraditional," however, is becoming less and less useful as a monolithic, homogeneous *student market* category, just as FPCU is less and less useful as a single *organizational* category. What are the emerging forms, manifestations, and niches of a nontraditional student that will become an increasingly attractive market for subsets of FPCUs? What are the characteristics of some of the markets that some FPCUs will pursue as the contexts of postsecondary education and workforce preparation become more complexly intertwined? What do the growing differences among FPCUs suggest about the markets of individual FPCUs? Do they help us to understand (even predict) the future behavior of individual firms over and above their recent past history? Individual firms seek to differentiate their products and services from those of their competitors, but to what extent are the differences more a reflection of an institution's historical "niche" and a reflection of its current circumstances than they are of intentional strategies that will more fundamentally distinguish them in the future?

Our goal here is to try to push beyond proliferating categories of postsecondary schooling provision described earlier and identify implicit markets that some FPCUs seem to be pursuing. These models imply the possibility of corporate strategies as FPCUs pursue profits through for service differentiation.

Individual FPCUs are pursuing one or more of at least five *extensions* of their historic markets. As a group, these markets are neither mutually exclusive nor collectively exhaustive. They also overlap to a considerable degree. Each, however, represents a relatively important dimension in the workings of at least *some* FPCUs, and the degree of importance varies greatly among *all* FPCUs.

1. The Employer, Not the Student, as the FPCU Market

This historic focus of FPCUs has been, and remains, the *employer as market*. In responding to labor demands of numerous employers, trades, and professions, FPCUs have and will largely continue to develop and offer programs that train students for positions where there is sufficient demand, and for which the investment in schooling is likely to be "recoverable" with increased wages that graduates can accrue. Yes, FPCUs recruit *students* who enroll largely to acquire skills and knowledge that will enhance their employment prospects, but the *programs* that FPCUs create and roll out across multiple campuses in high-demand labor markets are more in response to the demands of employers than to those of potential students.

Employer groups (e.g., large firms, occupational specialty groups, associations, regional employer boards) are involved with FPCUs in student recruitment and support, curriculum revision, faculty identification and recruitment, and graduate placement. The market is *not* the student in the traditional sense. Rather than listening largely to student interests as such, these FPCUs listen to changes in the demand for and supply of qualified employees across a range of labor categories—changes revealed or suggested by employers and employer-related organizations.

The key "driver" in this model is the explicit connection between changes in the quantity and quality of skills supplied by higher education in a region and changes in the number of jobs requiring those skills in that region. No job growth in a particular occupational category or industry means no growth in the related career-preparation programs offered by FPCUs. For example, the overall business performance of Lincoln Technical Institute, which offers programs in automotive maintenance (www.lincolnedu.com), is subject to the overall business performance of the automotive industry (Gubins, 2008). DeVry University, a company heavily focused on information technology programs, provided a more dramatic illustration of this connection. Between 2001 and 2005, its enrollments fell to 38,083 from a peak of 49,481—due largely, it is argued, to the misfortunes of the dot-com industry at the time (Garrett, 2005).

Although FPCUs historically listen to employers, students themselves are increasingly opting for career-oriented majors at TCUs as well as at FPCUs (Astin, 1998). Furthermore, it turns out that when students select career-oriented curricula at *any* postsecondary institution, they tend to move more expeditiously into the work world. Based on research from the Institute of Educational Sciences, about two-thirds of all undergraduate majors in 1992–1993 had "career-oriented" content, relative to the one-third who had "academic content" (Choy, Bradburn, & Carroll, 2008). Ten years after graduation, "[t]he work experiences of graduates with academic and career-oriented majors differed, with career-oriented majors appearing to become established in the workforce earlier" (Choy, Bradburn, & Carroll, 2008, p. iii). Broadly speaking, programs with career intent appear to have a demonstrable effect on subsequent employment.

Continued growth in this FPCU market has four characteristics.

First, the number and nature of FPCU career programs is proliferating. How? The number of occupational categories continues to expand. It is not strictly accurate to say that the era of the neighborhood welding school run by its owner is ending (NEA Higher Education, 2004), because welding is still offered as part of hundreds of programs across the country. In addition to expanding programs around longstanding occupational categories such as welding, cosmetology, and accounting, FPCUs are also creating programs around relatively new and emerging occupational fields as diverse as computer game design and criminal justice (Garrett, 2005).

Second, FPCUs are also differentiating themselves on the degree to which they are "moving up-market" both in occupational titles and in degree levels. To the growing variety of skilled trades, FPCUs have been adding technical and professional programs, especially large-scale occupations with high prospects for employability. FPCUs continue to anchor their historic "lower" end of the certificate and degree hierarchy (i.e., nondegree, short courses, associate's degrees). However, over the last several decades, some FPCUs have added more degrees, higher degrees, graduate degrees, professional degrees, and terminal degrees.

This movement up the degree hierarchy corresponds, roughly, to the entry of FPCUs into occupational categories and fields that have historically been offered by TCUs, including programs in engineering, medicine, law, nursing, and education. Their growth in the field of education is illustrative. Before 1970, virtually all degree programs for educators were provided by TCUs. By the turn of the century, however, a number of FPCUs had developed a wide variety of programs for educators at the undergraduate, and especially the graduate, level (e.g., the Apollo Group, Capella Education, Walden University, Argosy University, the Education Management Corporation, the Career Education Corporation, Kaplan University) (Blumenstyk, 2003).

Capella University is emblematic of this recent, rapid, and diversifying growth in the education of educators. Capella did not exist prior to 1990. In 1993, it received approval to grant M.S. and Ph.D. degrees in education. Today it offers sixteen specializations at the master's degree level and sixteen specializations at the Ph.D. level. It has regional accreditation from the North Central Association of Colleges and Schools and currently enrolls over 23,000 undergraduate and graduate students across all programs of the university (Capella University, 2008). About 40% of their enrollments are Ph.D. or doctor of psychology students, many of whom are enrolled in education specialties. In these basic metrics, the education programs at Capella University are larger in enrollment size, greater in number, and higher in degree level than the majority of departments, schools, and colleges of education at TCUs. As a collection of institutions that have evolved over the last three decades, FPCUs are now producing more graduates from more career-oriented programs that are longer and at higher degree levels, and as a group are addressing a wider variety of careers.

2. Competing With TCUs Over the Student Market

FPCUs are also pursuing increasing proportions of students that have been nominally served by TCUs. This suggests that FPCUs and TCUs are beginning to compete more directly—due to at least two trends discussed earlier: *both* TCUs and FPCUs are providing more career-oriented programming, and FPCUs are providing more career-oriented programming (and at degree levels corresponding to TCUs) in fields historically dominated by TCUs. To the degree that TCUs have served largely the market of traditional students (18- to 22-year olds), some FPCUs may be pursuing these more traditional students. But this age cohort of students represents a declining share at most TCUs as well as FPCUs. It is probably more accurate to describe the competition between TCUs and FPCUs as being for *nontraditional* students rather than for traditional students. Without necessarily abandoning their historic career-related, short-duration, nondegree programs, some FPCUs are beginning to shift toward longer, more degree-based programs and, in some instances, programs that have broader, less occupation-specific emphases—programs that are more directly comparable to those offered by and in competition with TCUs.

Most of this growth, however, has been at the subbachelor's level. In the view of the Accrediting Commission of Career Schools and Colleges (ACCSC), the organization that is arguably best positioned to view these trends, there has been a steady increase in new program and degree program applications over the course of the last several years. These programs are also longer, on average—from twelve months in 2004 to thirteen months in 2005. The addition of associate's degrees has been one of the fastest growing segments of ACCSC accredited institutions. To the extent that more FPCUs are directly competing with TCUs, the primary point of competition seems to be at the associate's degree level and, to a lesser extent, professional school programs at multiple graduate degree levels.

Although FPCU–TCU competition can be inferred by a growing similarity of degree-level programs between them, actual head-to-head competition is more difficult to ascertain with precision. Without first-hand information from consumers on their alternatives and their individual choices, information on direct competition between FPCUs and TCUs can only be indirectly ascertained but not directly asserted. Why not? Changes in relative market share can be driven by a wide range of factors. Direct competition (conscious consumer choice) may or may not exist among entire sectors, among institutions, and among programs within institutions. Without information on conscious consumer choices, it is difficult to ascertain the relevance of possible comparative advantages like convenience, perceived program quality, and price.

One study of the loss of market share at one community college, however, reveals the possible effects of some FPCUs on some TCUs in one region of the country. It was conducted with the explicit aim of ascertaining the nature of competition facing one TCU—Northern Virginia Community College (Gabriel, 2005). While the population in Northern Virginia, including the number of students graduating from high schools, had increased over the fourteen years prior to the study, enrollment at NVCC grew at a slower than expected rate. Within a seventy-five-mile radius of the campus, a total of forty-six institutions of higher education were examined to compare their relative growth rates: twenty-one FPCUs and twenty-five TCUs, made up of thirteen public community colleges and twelve nonprofit four-year institutions. On average, enrollment increased from 1999 to 2003 by 15.9% at two-year TCUs and by 15.6% at four-year TCUs. At three of the FPCUs (i.e., Strayer University, The University of Phoenix, ITT Technical Institute), enrollment increased by an average of 92.3% (Gabriel, 2005) During the same period, enrollment at Northern Virginia Community College increased by only 1.1%.

These vastly differing growth rates raised a host of more detailed questions about possible causes associated with perceived program content and quality, placement effectiveness, price, opportunity cost, and convenience. Consider, for illustration, differences in price, how price changes affect demand, and several directly comparable program factors. At the end of the four-year period studied, average annual tuition at two-year TCUs stood at $2,306; at four-year TCUs, $14,144; and at FPCUs, $12,657. Over the four-year period, NVCC's tuition increased by 63.2%, from $935 to $1,526 per year, the lowest level (and the highest rate of increase) among the institutions studied. By contrast, Strayer University tuition was more than six times higher, at $391.50 per credit hour. How directly do these institutions compete? Of the forty-six institutions examined, about half (twenty-one, predominantly FPCUs) concentrate on one or a few focused career-training programs that appear to directly compete with those at NVCC: nine in continuing education or business, six in technical or computer training, and six in medical assistant training.

The competing programs of FPCUs offer a variety of scheduling options and also target potential students in nearby military installations. Compared to NVCC, they offered more evening classes (e.g., DeVry, ECPI College of Technology, Lincoln Technical Institute), both evening and weekend classes (e.g., Sanz School), courses online (e.g., University of Phoenix, Strayer, DeVry, ECPI, ITT Technical Institute), and special military programs or scholarships (e.g., Strayer University, ECPI College of Technology, ITT Technical Institute) (Gabriel, 2005).

To get a more focused view of competition, analysts reduced the scope of analysis to a seven-mile radius from a seventy-five-mile radius around NVCC. Seven FPCUs lie within the seven-mile radius, and the combined enrollment at five of these campuses increased from 1,100 in fall 2001 to 1,607 in fall 2002, a 46.1% increase in contrast to NVCC's 1.1% increase between 1999 and 2003 (Gabriel, 2005).

These data may suggest the possibility of FPCUs successfully competing against TCUs in the community college category, but they do not report the choices faced by individual students. They do, however, suggest differences in the relative importance attached to these particular programs by the competing institutions. Community colleges pursue multiple missions, only one of which is employee training. NVCC may, for example, place a much higher priority on its transfer mission than on its employee-training mission. Indeed, current levels of employee training at community colleges may, in the view of some, already be "too much":

> Public policy, while encouraging broader community college and industry partnership in employee training, must also *move to counteract* the harmful impacts of extensive employee training on other missions of the community college such as transfer preparation, remedial education, and general education. (Dougherty, 2003, p. 62)

The single-mission focus of FPCUs, in contrast to the multiple independent missions of TCUs, may explain a good part of the differences in employment training outcomes between these direct competitors. Yet, if community colleges claim employment training as one of their missions, then it is reasonable to compare changes in market share of its employment training programs over time.

Direct competition between FPCUs and TCUs is not limited to careers in the skilled trades. As mentioned earlier, professional school programs at TCUs are increasingly finding analogues among FPCUs. This FPCU market is, then, the students who have historically been served by TCUs in programs that are at the points of closest adjacency to FPCUs—i.e., in degree-denominated career preparation programs. Where numbers of jobs are large and compensation is sufficient to attract students to invest, FPCUs are developing new programs to serve these markets, despite the fact that TCUs have offered similar programs for years.

3. *"Partnering" With TCUs to Pursue a Common Student Market*

Direct competition between some FPCUs and TCUs does not preclude collaboration and other forms of partnering between FPCUs and TCUs. Partnering can and does include a wide variety of formal working relationships that bind one or more FPCUs to one or more TCUs, ranging from memoranda of understanding on student transfer of credits all the way to acquisitions and mergers. At the extreme end of that continuum, FPCUs acquire TCUs to gain access to new markets, academic programs, increased capabilities (e.g., online delivery), and licensing (e.g., accreditation). While partnerships are very often created by one firm to take advantage of strengths of the other firm, they are usually not thought of as requiring outright acquisition of the other firm. Whether acquisitions constitute partnerships is debatable, and our focus here is on those arrangements between FPCUs and TCUs wherein both types continue as autonomous entities, albeit with formal collaborative relationships. Each institution's goals are enhanced by working collaboratively with the other, suggesting that both institutions benefit by providing agreed-upon services to a *common pool* of students. This is the opposite of the previous, zero-sum model above, whereby a particular student is captured by one type of institution to the loss of the other institution.

Using this restrictive definition—"retained autonomy in the pursuit of a common pool of students"—we find FPCUs pursuing partnership agreements with TCUs that are, in effect, various forms of articulation agreements, broadly defined. "Articulation" currently runs more *from* TCUs *to* FPCUs than *to* TCUs *from* FPCUs—many TCUs are still reluctant to accept credits from FPCUs—but agreements exist in both directions and include more than articulation between formal degree programs. As one illustration, FPCUs are providing "pathway programs" to TCUs in which they recruit and educate foreign students in college-preparatory programs.

Over the past decade such partnerships "have become commonplace in [non-U.S.] English-speaking countries. About 20% of Australia's foreign students come into the country through these preparatory, or pathways, programs" (Fischer, 2008, p. 1). In the United States, Oregon State University has partnered with Navitas to provide such a program. Currently, Navitas has similar partnership arrangements with twenty-two universities worldwide. Typically it creates a separate, year-long program, usually housed on the TCU campus. Tuition varies based on the course of study but is often comparable to the fees paid by international students enrolled as undergraduates. The company incurs the cost of the program's marketing, recruitment, and operational costs, while the TCU provides classroom and office space. Students pay tuition to Navitas, which in turn gives the university a cut of 20–30%, depending on the course of study (Fischer, 2008).

Kaplan, Inc., has similar partnership arrangements with five British TCUs (Fischer, 2008) and has created a similar program with Northeastern University. A British FPCU, Into University Partnerships (www.into.uk.com/home), establishes partnerships with TCUs that take on the character of joint ventures. The partner university and IUP each put up resources for the program and agree to split the profit from fees paid by the pathways students. Labor relationships vary among these partnerships. TCU language instructors remain employees of the TCU in some cases; in others, both current instructors and those hired to handle the expanding workload are employees of the joint venture, or of the FPCU.

Just as pathway programs illustrate articulation *from* FPCUs *to* TCUs, degree transfer characterizes articulation *from* TCUs *to* FPCUs—for example, associate's degree programs at TCUs to bachelor's degree programs at FPCUs. Some of these even connect *nondegree* (certificate) students at TCUs to degree programs at FPCUs. The Extension Division of the University of California at Irvine, for example, has an articulation agreement with Capella University whereby Capella pays Irvine $500 for each student referred by UCI (Urdan, 2007). Students completing one of eight certificate programs at UCI become eligible for consideration in one of eight degree programs offered by Capella University.

Formal degree articulation, especially between associate's and bachelor's degree levels, is perhaps the partnership form with the largest potential. While bachelor's degree–granting TCUs have been generally reluctant to grant transfer credit earned at FPCUs, some associate's degree–granting TCUs have found it advantageous to partner with FPCUs to improve the transfer opportunities of their associate's degree graduates. Some of the arrangements have unusual features. The articulation partnership between

Linn-Benton Community College in Oregon and the University of Phoenix, for example, entails UOP physically locating a branch on the Linn-Benton campus. Both Phoenix and DeVry have created technologically oriented bachelor's of science degree programs that capitalize on TCU technical associate's-degree programs and that extend the number of credit hours that can be transferred beyond those that are typically granted by four-year TCUs (Blumenstyk, 2003). Community colleges that enter into similar agreements with Phoenix are able to jointly enroll their students at UOP, giving them immediate access to the university's online library and academic counseling services. They are also given access to the online programs that Phoenix uses to provide pedagogical training to its 7,000 instructors, as well as access to online student proficiency tests and remedial education programs (Blumenstyk, 2003). "Noncompete" clauses are often part of the partnership agreements, such as the stipulation that the FPCU will grant "junior status" only to students who have completed their associate's degree. Also, in some agreements the FPCU also agrees not to offer lower-division courses.

Partnering arrangements exist only when there are sufficient incentives at *both* TCUs and FPCUs. TCUs whose programs are at capacity may have little incentive to increase applicants. FPCUs, on the other hand, seek to grow their capacity, so they have incentives to increase student flows into their degree programs and on to programs beyond their degree levels. Growth through this channel will likely be with those TCUs that, like FPCUs, have incentives to increase student flows into and "up from" their programs.

4. Extending the Market "Downward" to Include High Schools

While the overall movement of FPCUs has been to add degrees to certificate programs and to add higher degrees to lower degree programs, some have moved in the other direction—toward compulsory schooling. The largest "falloff" in enrollments occurs at the transition between high school and college. Many, if not most, FPCUs have developed programs for high school *graduates* through which they seek to bridge the "gap" between high school graduation and successful entry into college. Recently, however, several FPCUs have taken steps to anchor themselves more firmly on both sides of that bridge by direct entry into K–12 schooling. Examples include both private pay and free or publicly funded models.

Kaplan University High School illustrates the private pay model. Kaplan Virtual Education, a subsidiary of Kaplan, Inc., has opened Kaplan University High School (www.kuhighschool.com), a private pay, online national high school where students have the option of enrolling in single courses or in an eighteen-credit "College Access Diploma" program (Urdan, 2007). KUHS is regionally accredited by the Southern Association of Colleges and Schools to award high school diplomas. After graduating from KUHS, students are free to apply to those postsecondary institutions that require a high school diploma, but they have an extra incentive to continue their education specifically at Kaplan University. The primary incentive is in the form of a tuition scholarship, whose terms and conditions are as follows:

> [A] partial scholarship entitles KU High School graduates to a 20% tuition discount on their Kaplan University tuition. To be eligible for the scholarship, a KU High School graduate must remain continuously enrolled as a full-time or part-time student in an associate's, or higher, degree program at Kaplan University and must successfully complete the program and receive the degree. Failure to maintain continuous enrollment will result in loss of the scholarship. Tuition discount not valid with any other scholarships, promotions, or savings program. (www.kuhighschool.com)

Insight Schools, a recent acquisition of the Apollo Group, illustrates the public (no tuition charges) model. Insight Schools (www.insightschools.net) partners with local communities and school districts to build and operate their online schools. They launched their first school in 2006 in Washington State. As a public school, the program is tuition-free to students who reside in Washington. Students in grades 9–12 can select from six academic tracks (e.g., advanced placement, college prep, foundations, English as a second language). Like the University of Phoenix, Insight Schools markets directly to families, as opposed to providing content and services to school districts. No formal incentives have yet been created to encourage Insight Schools graduates to continue their education at the University of Phoenix or UOP's online division, but those can reasonably be expected to emerge over time.

Other FPCUs have developed their own versions of these models. DeVry, Inc., purchased a virtual high school recently, and Capella University is sponsoring a newly-created charter high school in northern Minnesota (Urdan, 2007). The K–12 marketplace is generally less attractive than the postsecondary marketplace (Urdan, 2007), but the ability to connect directly with students prior to college makes this move more attractive than it might otherwise appear.

FPCUs' movement into compulsory schooling is, in retrospect, a natural extension of their historical pursuit of nontraditional college students. These are students (a) for whom the FPCU will be their first (and perhaps only) post-secondary experience and (b) for whom subsequent schooling may follow (but is not assured). These programs provide a combination of a completed program (i.e., high school) and increased likelihood of transitioning into and completing a post-secondary program. These programs *in FPCUs* are distinctive in that they address *both* high school completion and entry into postsecondary education. There are many students who might conceivably benefit from these bridging programs.

These are students' first institutions, providing foundational programs, that among other things, encourage vertical transfer for completion or additional degrees. By focusing attention on students who, for whatever reasons, are otherwise less likely to pursue higher education, this business model in effect seeks out and provides students who are at the beginning of their student lives in higher education, regardless of their age. They provide coursework that is an end in itself, usually leading to enhanced employability, but that is also transferable to the higher-level programs of other providers.

This market is generally problematic for a combination of reasons. Increasing numbers of marginal students elect FPCUs as their first-choice institution in order to obtain entry-level skills needed to enter the workforce. So far, so good. However, when these same students seek to continue their education, especially at a TCU, "they are often informed that the credit earned from their previous education [at an FPCU] is not transferable" (McComis, 2005, p. 1). Reluctance, largely on the part of TCUs, to accept transfer credits from FPCUs mitigates the ability of individual FPCUs to fully pursue this business model. To the extent that these restrictive practices become publicly viewed as detrimental to student access and attainment in higher education, TCUs may come under increased scrutiny and pressure from accrediting organizations, higher education associations, and state and federal agencies.

In the absence of universally accepted, multilateral transfer agreements on courses and programs, many TCUs have relied on the distinction of an institution's accreditation agency as a basis for determining whether to accept transfer credits. Specifically, they are willing to accept courses from a regionally accredited institution, but not from a nationally accredited institution—a practice of ambiguous rationale. FPCUs that succeed in getting their students' coursework transferable to TCUs will have a comparative advantage over those that do not, which will enable them to more effectively pursue the high school market.

5. Knitting Together Fragmented Student Coursework

Degree completion in American higher education is fundamentally driven by pre-determined systems of courses and credits. Responsibility and authority for framing programs, assembling and offering courses, assessing student progress, and granting degrees rests with institutions, but navigating through these systems across courses, programs, and institutions, as well as accumulating the right courses in the successful pursuit of the right certificates or degrees, often falls to students, with varying degrees of success. Some FPCUs become particularly adept at serving students with complex, incomplete, and disjointed academic histories, helping them aggregate and channel those histories into academic work that can count toward degree or program completion.

Enrollment in higher education is increasingly becoming unpackaged or unbundled. The characterization of a student enrolling in one institution to begin a program and staying in that program and institution through to graduation is fading, to be replaced by all manner of more fluid, flexible, and "noncomplete" alternatives. To illustrate, consider the fragmentation *after three academic years* of three pools of recent high school graduates who first enrolled in college in the fall of 2003.

1. Among those enrolled full time at four-year institutions and had bachelor's degree plans, 70% were still enrolled at their first institutions without a degree, 4% had attained a degree or certificate, 20% had transferred elsewhere without a degree, and 7% had left without a degree or certificate and did not enroll anywhere else within three years (Berkner & He, 2007).

2. Among *independent* students enrolled at four-year institutions, 50% had not attained any degree and were no longer enrolled, 41% had not attained any degree but were still enrolled, 5% had attained a degree or certificate and were still enrolled, and 5% had attained a degree or certificate and were no longer enrolled (Berkner & He, 2007).

3. Among those enrolled in public two-year institutions full-time with associate's degree plans, 23% attained an associate's degree at that institution, 31%

were still enrolled there without a degree, 24% had transferred elsewhere without a degree, and 21% had not attained any degree at the first institution and did not enroll anywhere (Berkner & He, 2007).

As implied, large proportions of students in higher education do not complete programs at the institutions where they began, if at all. As they pursue their education, many find themselves in various states of noncompletion. In addition to *vertical* transfer (i.e., from a two-year to a four-year college), students pursue *horizontal* transfer among both similar and nonsimilar IHEs, attend more than one IHE at a time, and, as a result, face problems transferring their course credits and aggregating them into certificates and degrees. The net result is a loss of aggregate achievement on the part of both the students and of the institutions they attended.

Indicators suggesting growth in transfers are anecdotal, but they emanate from a variety of sources and all point in the same upward direction (Council for Higher Education Accreditation Committee on Transfer and the Public Interest, 2000). The majority of 1996 baccalaureate graduates attended at least two colleges and universities. Many students taking distance learning courses are enrolled in another institution different from the distance learning providers. Students attending corporate universities and certain unaccredited institutions are seeking to transfer their coursework to accredited institutions. Increasing numbers of students are enrolling in foreign institutions and seeking to transfer credits into American colleges and universities. Increasing numbers of virtual institutions and corporate providers, along with FPCUs, are forming partnerships with TCUs to offer courses and programs.

The issues associated with credit transfer and credit equivalency between any two institutions are several, often involving sector locations, accreditation status, and institutional evaluation consistency, as well as the more obvious content and program relevance of individual courses.

The reinforcing trends of new FPCU providers and increasing transfers raise to a level of prominence the degree to which an FPCU can provide students the service of aggregating, aligning, and, in effect, repurposing prior coursework toward certificates and degrees offered by that institution. FPCUs bundle courses taken elsewhere and, with academic counseling and guidance, help students purposefully package them into a certificate or degree. Such services are provided at about 85% of two-year and about 95% of four-year FPCUs (Chronicle of Higher Education, 2008).

Conclusion

These five new markets are more accurately described as extensions of the nontraditional student market. FPCUs continue to serve these students, but, with decades of growth, have extended their reach into the higher education marketplace. Having effectively tripled their share of the postsecondary education market in recent decades, FPCUs are now extending their pursuit of nontraditional students by (a) reaching further into the workplace for new programs to attract them, (b) moving "up-market" to compete directly with TCUs for them, (c) partnering with TCUs to "share" them, (d) more intentionally servicing the students for whom the FPCU would be their first, but not last, postsecondary experience, and (e) and focusing more intentionally on students who have bounced around higher education with little cumulative coherence in their experience before enrolling in an FPCU. The future evolution of FPCU programs and markets is more than a story of growth— it reflects an emerging variety of pathways to reach and serve nontraditional students with postsecondary career-focused programming.

References

Astin, A. (1998). The changing American college student: Thirty-year trends, 1966–1996, *The Review of Higher Education, 21*(2), 115–135.

Berkner, L., & He, S. (2007). *Persistence and attainment of 2003–4 beginning postsecondary students: After three years (NCES 2007–169)*. National Center for Education Statistics, Institute of Education Sciences, U.S. Department of Education. Washington, DC. Retrieved November 3, 2007, from http://nces.ed.gov/pubsearch.

Blumenstyk, G. (2003, September 5). Companies' graduate programs challenge colleges of education, for-profit institutions find a new market: Schoolteachers. *Chronicle of Higher Education.* Retrieved August 22, 2008, from http://chronicle.com/prm/weekly/v50/802/02a0300a.htm.

Borden, V. M. H., Brown, P. C., & Majesky-Pullmann, O. (2007). Top 100 undergraduate degree producers: Interpreting the data. *Diverse Issues in Higher Education, 24*(8), 21–29, 31–45, 37–61.

Brewer, D., Gates, S., & Goldman, C. A. (2002). *In pursuit of prestige: Strategy and competition in U.S. higher education.* Piscataway, NJ: Transaction Publishers.

Capella University. (2008). Programs by degree. Retrieved August 20, 2008, from www.capella.edu/default.aspx.

Choy, S., Bradburn, E., & Carroll, C. D. (2008). *Ten years after college: Comparing the employment experiences of 1992–93 bachelor's degree recipients with academic and career-oriented majors.* Washington, DC: Institution for Education Sciences, National Center for Education Statistics.

Christensen, C. M. (2007). *The innovator's dilemma: When new technologies cause great firms to fail.* Cambridge, MA: Harvard Business School Press.

Christensen, C. M., Horn, M. B., & Johnson, C. W. (2008). *Disrupting class: How disruptive innovation will change the way the world learns.* New York: McGraw-Hill.

Christensen, C. M., & Raynor, M. E. (2003). *The innovator's solution: Creating and sustaining successful growth.* Cambridge, MA: Harvard Business School Press.

Chronicle of Higher Education (2008). *The Chronicle Almanac, 2007–8.* Washington, DC: Chronicle of Higher Education.

Council for Higher Education Accreditation Committee on Transfer and the Public Interest (2000). *A statement to the community: Transfer and the public interest.* Washington, DC: Author.

Dougherty, K. J. (2003). The uneven distribution of employee training by community colleges: Description and explanation. *ANNALS of the American Academy of Political and Social Science 586,* 62–91.

Fischer, K. (2008, June 20). All abroad! Overseas study required. *Chronicle of Higher Education.* Retrieved September 25, 2008, from http://chronicle.com/weekly/V54/i41/41a00101.htm.

Gabriel, G. (2005). *Growth of proprietary schools in the Northern Virginia area.* (Research Report No. 15-05). Annandale, VA: Office of Institutional Research, Northern Virginia Community College.

Garrett, R. (2005). *The Global Education Index: 2005, Part 2: Public companies— relationships with nonprofit higher education.* London: The Observatory on Borderless Higher Education.

Goan, S. K., & Cunningham, A. F. (2007). *Differential characteristics of 2-year postsecondary institutions.* Washington, DC: National Center for Education Statistics, U.S. Department of Education.

Gubins, S. (2008, March 10). Education conference highlights: Focus on lending. *Education and Training Services Bi-Weekly: Industry Overview,* p. 22.

JBL Associates. (2003). *A profile of career colleges and universities: Fact book 2003.* Washington, DC: Career Training Foundation.

JBL Associates, & Wilson, H. (2007). *Economic impact of America's career colleges.* Washington, DC: Imagine America Foundation.

JBL Associates. (2008). *2008 Fact book: A profile of career colleges and universities.* Washington, DC: Imagine America Foundation.

McComis, M. S. (2005). *Transfer of credit: A policy agenda.* Washington, DC: Accrediting Commission of Career Schools and Colleges of Technology.

National Education Association. (2004). Proprietary education: Threat or not? *NEA Higher Education, 1*(1), 1–6.

Silber, J. M. (2006). *Equity research: Education and training.* New York: BMO Capital Markets.

Tierney, W. G., & Hentschke, G. C. (2007). *New players, different game: Understanding the rise of for-profit colleges and universities.* Baltimore, MD: Johns Hopkins University Press.

Urdan, T. (2007). K–12 heating up. *Education Signals, 2*(18), 2–3.

3

WHO ARE THEY? AND WHAT DO THEY DO?

Vicente M. Lechuga

The proliferation of for-profit degree-granting colleges and universities over the last decade has brought with it numerous questions about whether profit-seeking motives can peacefully coexist with the dissemination of knowledge. While it is safe to assume that for-profit colleges and universities (FPCUs) are in fact providing students with the knowledge and skill sets needed to succeed in the current job market, critics argue that FPCUs do not provide the kind of "knowledge" available to students at public and private nonprofit colleges and universities—i.e., education that focuses on personal development rather than specific skills. Instead, they provide in-depth instruction and practical information that meets the needs of employers and the job market. Said differently, the former provides students with an "education," while the latter provides them with training. Moreover, the argument continues, if what students at FPCUs receive is indeed a "traditional" education, then those who provide that education may not have the requisite training and skills to do so. Similarly, these faculty members may not have sufficient expertise to determine what should be taught.

Such arguments are predicated on the notion that seeking profits by educating students is detrimental to our higher education system. In other words, because the profit-seeking behavior of FPCUs focuses on efficiency and cost, both the curricula and faculty quality are compromised in favor of revenue generation. The issue at hand is less about the dissemination of knowledge itself, and instead concerns itself with the *type* of knowledge that is distributed, and *by whom*, when a profit-seeking motive exists within a postsecondary education structure.

In what follows, I present findings from a twelve-month study that examined faculty members and faculty culture at four distinct FPCUs. I begin by offering some background information about for-profit institutions to provide a context, and present the various characteristics that define faculty work life at these institutions. I highlight the differences that exist between institutions *within* the for-profit higher education realm and explore how those differences influence both the type of faculty that are employed and the roles they are expected to play. The chapter highlights the personal and professional characteristics that make up the faculty at each of the four institutions and examines their various roles and responsibilities. The paper also considers how FPCUs determine who their faculty members will be, the extent of their roles and responsibilities, and how such determinations are made. My goal is to offer an understanding of the faculty members who teach at for-profit postsecondary institutions that moves away from the common archetype used to describe who they are and what they do.

The Dynamic Nature of Faculty Work

Faculty roles and responsibilities have changed dramatically since the establishment of the first Colonial colleges. The seventeenth- and eighteenth-century Harvard tutors, for instance, were responsible for teaching the entire curriculum, which was religious and sectarian in nature (Rudolph, 1990). As the number of institutions increased and function and purpose of higher education began to change, so, too, did faculty work. After disciplines began to take hold in the late nineteenth century and research became an important function of the "multiversity," faculty roles and responsibilities once again changed accordingly (Kerr, 2001). Today, faculty members are employed by a wide array of postsecondary institutions ranging from doctoral institutions whose focus is on research and associates' colleges offer a two-year curriculum to special focus institutions that concentrate on a single field or related fields of study (Carnegie Foundation for the Advancement of Teaching, 2006). Each institutional type requires faculty to have a specific kind of educational training, disciplinary specialization, and set of work responsibilities. Faculty members employed by one type of institution would not necessarily be qualified to work at another. A skilled researcher and faculty member at a doctoral institution, for instance, may not be the best candidate to hire at a liberal arts college, which requires its faculty to be experts in the classroom. Said differently, faculty members are not a monolithic group of individuals that possess similar skills and abilities across all types of institutions. Rather, who they are and what they do varies depending on their specific institution, making it difficult to generalize about faculty members' major responsibilities. What is more, as the number of postsecondary institutions continues to increase—as do the number of nontraditional student populations—faculty members are being asked to acquire new skill sets to serve the various needs of an increasingly diverse group of students.

Following the end of World War II, for instance, formal academic life in the United States consisted of several facets categorized under teaching-related activities, service to the academic community, and research and publishing (Finkelstein, 1984). Traditional colleges and universities continue to favor this multifaceted vision of faculty work life. Yet, faculty members' priorities with regard to these various duties are a reflection of the norms and values of the institutions that employ them. At the nation's most prestigious universities, faculty members spend the majority of their time focusing on the latter. At less prestigious regional colleges, faculty may focus more of their efforts on the teaching rather than the research component of the profession.

The manner in which faculty work life has been defined in the literature (Austin, 1990; Becher, 1987; Clark, 1983; Tierney & Rhoades, 1993) overlooks the environments in which faculty at FPCUs work. Traditional notions of faculty work are constructed with the assumption that faculty members are full-time, tenure-track employees who are engaged in varying degrees of teaching, research, and service, depending on institutional type. The culture of the professorate is such that faculty work is presumed to take place in isolation; autonomy is a key characteristic that defines faculty work life (Austin, 1990). Faculty work is also framed within the context of traditional, nonprofit higher education institutions where shared governance is the norm and faculty members have input and decision making authority into several areas of the university. As will be discussed shortly, faculty members participating in this study do not fit this mold, in part because FPCUs have shifted the education paradigm that is familiar to those in traditional academe—specifically, the paradigm that centers faculty work life around notions of shared governance and collegiality.

New Skills

Innovations in higher education brought about significant changes in the ways faculty members go about their work in traditional and for-profit institutions. The Internet, for example, made online courses commonplace at a number of traditional colleges and universities, and many faculty members currently incorporate a Web-based component into their "on-ground" courses. The Internet also served as the impetus for a new wave of for-profit, regionally accredited online universities such as Capella University and Jones International University, both of which were founded in 1993. Large public research universities also have begun to offer online graduate degrees. The University of Maryland offers a master of life sciences degree as well as a professional master of engineering in fire protection degree, completely online. Boston University offers both a master's and doctorate in music education online as well.

Fewer Resources

Another important factor that contributes to the changing nature of faculty work life pertains to employment status. In seeking ways to cut costs, colleges and universities have turned to part-time and full-time contracted faculty to teach courses previously taught by full-time tenure track faculty members. Part-time faculty members provide an increasing amount of the instructional services at traditional colleges and universities; these faculty members make up over 43% of the professoriate (National Center for Education Statistics [NCES], 1998). Individuals appointed to part-time and contracted positions, by definition, are non–tenure-track faculty members. Part-time faculty generally earn no benefits and are paid a fraction of what their full-time tenured and tenure-track counterparts earn, comparatively. Statistics show that more than 50% of all new appointments in higher education are non-tenure-track hires, also known as off-track hires (American Association of University Professors [AAUP], 2003). Off-track hires were virtually unheard of 40 years ago, constituting only 3.3% of all full-time positions in 1969 (AAUP, 2003).

Colleges and universities hire part-time and full-time off-track faculty as money-saving tactics that allows administrators to keep full-time, tenured, and tenure-track faculty salaries competitive while maintaining low levels of tuition for students (Gappa & Leslie, 1993; Jacobs, 1998; Schuster & Finkelstein, 2006).

Traditional institutions continue to hire increasing numbers of part-time faculty due to institutional budget cuts resulting from decreasing state appropriations to higher education. The main controversy regarding contingent faculty centers on the idea that the nature of this type of appointment undermines the basic tenets of the academy—i.e., shared governance, tenure, and so forth. With the advent of for-profit postsecondary institutions, debates regarding a growing dependence on contingent faculty persist as their numbers continue to increase.

New Competitors

Although FPCUs comprise over one third of all postsecondary education institutions in the country, they enroll about 6% of the total student population (NCES, 2003). Just as traditional colleges and universities differ in size, type, and educational mission—community colleges versus research universities, for example—marked differences exist in the for-profit higher education sector. As such, the type of faculty that are employed and their specific roles and responsibilities will vary. To be sure, generalizations about for-profit colleges and universities can be made, but such comparisons need to be made with caution. To compare DeVry University with a local proprietary business college is akin to saying that an airplane and a bicycle are comparable modes of transportation.

Similarly, it would be unfair to equate faculty work at community colleges with that of faculty at research extensive universities; their responsibilities will differ greatly. Faculty at the former likely will have a much greater teaching load and little to no publishing requirements, while those employed at the latter will spend the majority of their time on research-related activities. In general, the function and purpose of traditional institutions will vary. By the same token, for-profit colleges and universities differ in mission and scope, and faculty members at one institution will not necessarily have similar roles and responsibilities as faculty at another.

There are a number of ways to categorize the types of for-profit colleges and universities. One method is to categorize them by ownership status (Kinser, 2006). The largest for-profit education providers are publicly traded conglomerates. These institutions are set up as corporations whose shares can be bought and sold on the open market. The University of Phoenix, which is owned and operated by the Apollo Group, is an example of one such entity.

However, publicly traded institutions like the University of Phoenix make up a small minority of the for-profit higher education market. Numerous FPCUs are privately held companies owned either by a single individual or family, or by a group of investors. Although the fiscal ramifications of ownership may differ, it is difficult to generalize whether or how it affects faculty work given the large number of privately held FPCUs.

An alternative taxonomy that can be utilized takes into consideration curricular offerings (Tierney & Hentschke, 2007). A number of FPCUs are designed to educate students for mid-level and senior management positions in such fields such as business and education. Others provide vocational training to students for numerous occupations such as HVAC (heating, ventilation, and air conditioning) technician, dental assistant, or administrative office manager. Many FPCUs offer academic programs at the associate's degree level, while others offer graduate and professional degrees. Differences in institutional type with regard to academic and curricular offerings should not be overlooked. First, these differences can significantly influence the roles, responsibilities, and modalities of faculty work. Second, they provide a context from which to critically examine the role that for-profit institutions, and the faculty they employ, play in the larger realm of higher education.

Scholars have begun to address numerous issues concerning for-profit institutions (Berg, 2004; Kirp, 2004; Pusser & Turner 2004; Washburn, 2005), yet it is critical for researchers not to overlook one important issue. Not all FPCUs are alike, and nor are their faculty. Large publicly traded for-profit institutions, such as the University of Phoenix, tend to be used as the archetype for all FPCUs. For example, it is not uncommon for scholars to point to a lack of faculty involvement in governance activities, a lack of control over the curriculum, and a limited amount of academic freedom as attributes that apply to all faculty members employed at for-profit institutions. While this may hold true for some, such blanket statements paint an inaccurate and monolithic image of for-profit postsecondary education providers and their faculty. Previous research (Lechuga, 2006) reveals clear differences in work responsibilities, educational levels, and participation in curricular and decision making activities, among others.

One segment of higher education that has experienced a dramatic increase in the number of institutions is the for-profit/proprietary sector (Education Commission of the States, 2000). Specifically, I am referring to the growth in the number of regionally accredited, degree-granting colleges and universities such as the University of Phoenix and numerous lesser-known institutions. The individuals that comprise the faculties at FPCUs are, on the one hand, similar to faculty at traditional institutions. There are significant differences, on the other hand, that critics often point to as weaknesses of for-profit institutions. Yet, these alternative educational providers are becoming commonplace in the previously banal realm of postsecondary education that is dominated by private nonprofit and public institutions (herein referred to as "traditional" institutions). For-profit colleges and universities no longer are at the fringes of the higher education realm. They are now a mainstay in higher education and will continue to expand the over $6 billion postsecondary education market.

In what follows, I offer data that will help to elucidate the various roles and responsibilities of faculty who work at FPCUs after providing readers with a brief summary of the study's research design. My intent is to provide readers with a new understanding of faculty members working in this sector of higher education so as to move away from the monolithic portrait of the roles and responsibilities faculty have. Some of the data show, for example, that faculty members have limited decision making authority—a widespread assumption about the manner in which FPCUs operate. Conversely, other data make clear that faculty at some institutions have a certain level of autonomy that allows them to create courses and curricula. The point here is to argue that a comprehensive understanding of the type of work faculty at FPCUs do is warranted to properly understand the function and purpose of these institutions.

Research Design

Data for this study were taken from a qualitative research project designed to explore faculty culture at for-profit institutions. The study included a total of fifty-two faculty members (twenty part-time and thirty-two full-time employees) from four different for-profit institutions that offered academic degree programs at the undergraduate and graduate levels. The term "for-profit institution" is narrowly defined here as a nationally or regionally accredited proprietary institution whose primary function is to provide postsecondary education to students and award academic degrees at either the undergraduate or graduate level. In many cases, these institutions offer certificates as well as degrees.

Participants were interviewed for 60 minutes and were guaranteed confidentiality. This helps to create an environment for participants that allowed them to answer questions about the challenges and barriers they faced. All the interviews were recorded and subsequently transcribed to facilitate in the coding process. Extensive notes were also taken during and after each interview. Participants answered questions from a standard protocol as well as other unscripted inquiries that emerged throughout the course of the interviews. Semistructured interviews allowed participants the freedom to direct the interview to places of importance to them. This data allowed for a thorough exploration of their roles and responsibilities. Data were organized and coded in a manner consistent with the issues and themes that arose during the initial analysis.

Data were analyzed using the constant-comparative method (Strauss & Corbin, 1990), allowing for the researcher to develop categories and themes as they arose during and after the data collection period. Codes were arranged into themes that provided insight into the responsibilities and composition of faculty bodies at the four FPCUs under study. Data were triangulated using techniques consistent with conventional qualitative research methods. Company reports, faculty handbooks, course syllabi, memos, and other documents were used to provide an alternative view of the data for reasons of reliability and trustworthiness.

Findings

One would assume that because FPCUs operate within a new educational paradigm, their instructional staffs would, to a great extent, differ in composition, background, and responsibilities from faculty at traditional colleges and universities. This is the case with regard to certain characteristics, but not others. To begin, I offer five areas that underscore the aspects of faculty composition and work life specific to the participating FPCUs, which are defined in Table 3.1: (1) diverse faculty bodies, (2) increased administrative authority, (3) institutional adaptability, (4) performance-based employment , and (5) academic constraints. The roles and responsibilities of faculty are explored within the context of the areas outlined here. Moreover, these areas shed light on how the context in which they work shapes their perspectives with regard to notions of shared governance, tenure, and academic freedom.

TABLE 3.1
Distinct Features of Faculty Work Life at FPCUs

Theme	Characterized By
Diverse faculty bodies	Level of education and types of degree programs differ by institution
Increased administrative authority	Contingent employment status, decreased level of participation in governance activities
Institutional adaptability	Quick decision making, responding to the needs of employers and the market
Performance-based employment	Good performance is rewarded; poor performance is not
Academic constraints	Inability to address working conditions, and limits on faculty input into the curriculum

Diverse Faculty Bodies

One of the most apparent distinctions between institutions participating in the study relates to the makeup of their faculty. The most obvious difference pertains to the type of faculty each type of institutions hires. For example, part-time faculty members made up over 90% of the instructional staffs at two of the four institutions. Data also show that, like traditional institutions, different types of FPCUs require different types of faculty. An associate's degree program in travel and tourism will require a different type of faculty than a master's degree in educational administration. Two of the institutions offered graduate-level degree programs and required faculty members to hold doctoral degrees. For the participants that taught in a doctoral level program, the institution sought faculty with extensive research and/or professional backgrounds in their specific discipline. Table 3.2 provides an overview of the faculty members at each institution, by highest level of education.

Level of education. Faculty members at traditional colleges and universities typically have similar levels of training and education. At the community college level, faculty are required to have a master's degree, but it is not uncommon to see many with Ph.D.s. By and large, traditional four-year institutions require faculty to have doctoral degrees. At FPCU No. 1, seventeen of the eighteen participants held doctorates; the eighteenth participant currently was pursuing a doctorate given that the institution focused on graduate-level degree programs. Consider also that thirteen participants had

TABLE 3.2
Highest Degrees Held by Faculty Participants, by Institution

Institution	Associate's	Bachelor's	Master's	Doctorate*	Doctorate in progress**
FPCU No. 1 (focused on master's and doctoral programs)	0	0	1	17	1
FPCU No. 2 (focused on bachelor's and master's programs)	0	0	10	5	2
FPCU No. 3 (focused on associate's programs)	1	6	0	1	0
FPCU No. 4 (focused on associate's and bachelor's programs)	0	2	8	1	0

*Juris Doctorate included
**These individuals also are included in the master's degree category

achieved or were currently pursuing tenure at a traditional institution. This institution made an effort to hire individuals from the traditional higher education ranks. "Over the last two or three years, [this university] has been hiring more academic type of people . . . because at the doctoral level you have the research requirement. So, [this university] is sort of strengthening the faculty with respect to their background."

Conversely, faculty members from the remaining three institutions were recruited from outside the education arena. "In order to teach at [this university] you have to be working in the area you are going to teach . . . that is one of the things we push pretty heavily at [this university]." FPCU No. 2 educational focus was on undergraduate and graduate training, with the majority of graduate programs at the master's degree level, as shown in Table 3.3. Faculty members were required to hold at least a master's degree.

TABLE 3.3
Number of Undergraduate and Graduate Degrees Offered,
by Level and Institution

Institution	Associate's	Bachelor's	Master's	Doctorate
FPCU No. 1				
(master's/doctoral programs)	0	2	6	7
FPCU No. 2				
(bachelor's/master's programs)	1	15	26	4
FPCU No. 3				
(associate's degree programs)	22	2	0	0
FPCU No. 4				
(associate's/bachelor's programs)	17	18	0	0

Nevertheless, five participants held doctorates (including a JD), and two were enrolled in doctoral programs at the time.

Types of programs. Not surprisingly, differences with regard to highest level of education were evident when comparing the types of programs the institutions offered. The number of bachelor's, master's, and doctoral degrees offered by the institution determined the level of education required of faculty. The majority of the faculty who taught at FPCU No. 1 held a terminal degree, given that most students were at the graduate level. Conversely, most faculty members at FPCU No. 3 did not hold a degree above the baccalaureate level, since the majority of their programs were two-year vocational degrees. These kinds of differences are not uncommon in traditional higher education when one considers the different educational levels between faculty members at a research university versus those who teach in vocational programs at community colleges.

Increased Administrative Authority

Faculty members who work at FPCUs are typically contract hires; tenure is non-existent with the exception of a handful of institutions across the country. For-profits have greater latitude in hiring and dismissing faculty members than do their counterparts at traditional institutions. Consequently, faculty authority is minimized, giving administrators greater discretion over policy issues. Administrators, for instance, were able to implement new practices that affect the classroom without consulting with their faculty. Such was the case when administrators decided that course readings and textbooks were to be available only online—referred to below as "resource."

> I am sure if my faculty had a vote, they would not have us going to resource because faculty, for the most part, like books. There are some decisions that are simply corporate decisions, and faculty won't have even a vote in that.

Full-time versus part-time. At FPCUs No. 1 and 2, full-time faculty consisted of less than 5% of the faculty body, and much of their responsibilities were administrative in nature. Many of their responsibilities centered on hiring, training, and evaluating part-time faculty members, with course instruction being minimal. One participant stated, "There really are no full-time faculty. There are full-time employees that also teach, but there are no full-time faculty." While it is fair to say that full-time faculty members are involved in decision making activities, one also can argue that these individuals hold positions that are comparable to administrative posts at traditional colleges and universities.

FPCUs No. 3 and 4 had a greater percentage of full-time faculty, but full-time faculty at these institutions held relatively little authority outside the curriculum. The majority of their decision making authority rested outside the faculty realm, which in one case, resulted in a great amount of tension between the two parties. Faculty, for example, were "encouraged" not to establish a faculty union or risk losing their jobs. "Our employment status is solely at the whim of the owner/president. If [a faculty union] were to be implemented, there would be a mass dismissal." With regard to creating a faculty union, another participant remarked, "One person owns the school. He doesn't want it, so therefore, it doesn't happen."

Business decisions. Increased administrative authority in the for-profit higher education sector is a result of the profit-seeking nature of the institutions. Participants described much of the administrative decision making activities as "business decisions." One participant stated with regard to the institution's decision making activities: "[they often] take a top-down approach [because] that's the way corporations are." In some instances faculty asserted that the business decision making model dominated, asserting, "Everything is a business decision."

Administrative decisions take into account both the academic and profit-seeking characteristics of the institution. "Business decisions" are not meant to suggest that academic quality is overlooked or compromised in favor of profits.

Rather, business decisions strive to maintain a balance between quality and profits. FPCUs attempt to maximize profits while maintaining a desired level of educational quality. While profits are obviously important to the institution, quality was also an entrenched value of the FPCUs participating in the study.

To be sure, individuals whose experience lay in the realm of business and the market ought to make the majority of the decisions that require such expertise. Faculty members at for-profit institutions may not necessarily be the most qualified individuals within the organization to make business decisions and therefore are often excluded from the process. As one faculty member stated, "It's pretty easy on my level, I do not have any voice on the business side of things, and it's just that simple. I am aware that it exists." Yet, the previous comments also illustrate how faculty members are excluded from the decision making. "Sometimes [decisions] are done for business reasons, you know. And sometimes it's 'Well, why did they do that?' Well, there's a reason, you know."

General differences between faculty participation in governance activities are evident, as summarized in Table 3.4. A system of shared governance, as exemplified at traditional institutions, is non-existent. Although decision making activities are shared between faculty members and administrators, a large proportion of the decision making authority resides outside the faculty domain. Faculty participation in governance activities is minimized, resulting in increased administrative authority.

Institutional Adaptability

As previously mentioned, FPCUs do not operate within the parameters of a system of shared governance, which results in limited faculty involvement in

TABLE 3.4
Faculty Participation in Various Types of Governance Activities at Traditional vs. For-Profit Colleges and Universities

Governance Activities	Traditional IHEs	For-Profit IHEs
Develop own courses	Yes	Varies by institution
Design curriculum/programs	Yes	Limited participation
Admissions decisions	Yes	No
Faculty hiring/firing decisions	Yes	Limited input
Faculty promotion decisions	Yes	No

decision making—much of which is predetermined by the administration. Shared decision making is connected to the (traditional) university's unique mission of creating and disseminating knowledge (AAUP, 2001); yet the paradigm in which FPCUs operate does not include research and knowledge production as a function of these institutions. Thus a system of shared governance is not warranted. Nevertheless, when faculty members are limited in their ability to govern, questions arise about the motives that drive institutional decisions and their effect on educational quality.

All four institutions promote faculty participation in decision making activities, but their governance structures are such that decisions, including those that directly affect academic quality, are made by a few individuals; many have corporate backgrounds. For example, the decision to offer new degree programs is often made outside the faculty realm. "To get a program approved, there are many different people looking at it. And in the end, it's truly a business decision." Another faculty member explained,

> If your profits go down to an unacceptable level, you are going to do something about it, and that is still a little bit different than the kind of bottom-line discussions that happen, I think, in [traditional] private and public institutions.

Flexible organizations. The governance structures of for-profit institutions are intended to promote swift decision making. Decisions regarding the institution can be made quickly because fewer individuals are involved in the process. In addition, decision making involves external constituencies, such as program advisory boards. This type of governance structure has both positive and negative consequences.

On the positive side, for-profit institutions are able to quickly adapt to the external environment and the changing needs of the market. They are able to assess the needs of employers and students and design courses and programs that fit those needs. Since fewer individuals are involved in the process, FPCUs are able to make decisions about which academic programs to offer and which to close. A faculty member commented that while the decision making process at traditional institutions favors inclusion, it is cumbersome and unable to respond as quickly to the needs of the market. "My colleagues and friends that I have in more traditional educational institutions get very frustrated sometimes with the pace of change. It just crawls. By the time it gets to where it needs to, some things have passed." Another provided an additional example that demonstrates the difference in decision making abilities.

> X University, here in [the city], is a great institution. There are some marvelous people there. They've been putting together the Management College, probably for about five years. It still hasn't started. They have a dean, they have funding, and they've done a fabulous job raising money. But they haven't taught one student. I mean, we would have changed it five times in that length of time.

For-profit institutions are able to adapt to meet the needs of the changing educational environment, but to do so requires decreased levels of faculty involvement in the decision making process. Consequently, when faculty involvement in the decision making process is minimized, decision making activities can be regarded negatively by individuals who are accustomed to faculty involvement in the process. Critics of for-profit education often point to the tension between education and profit as an element that can damage the quality of an education.

Performance-Based Employment Security

Without the protection of tenure or a faculty union, job security was viewed differently. With the exception of faculty members from FPCU No. 1 (most of whom came from traditional academe), participants came from professional backgrounds and were accustomed to the notion of job security as a function of one's ability to perform well. Not surprisingly, a number of the participants' perceptions of tenure were cynical. "Tenured positions are often viewed as a panacea by those who seek to rest upon their accomplishments of yesteryear." In other cases, the lack of tenure was not a factor for faculty members who chose to teach at a for-profit institution. "I don't think tenure is an issue. If tenure were important to you, you wouldn't come to work at a place that doesn't have tenure." Whether an institution offered tenure was irrelevant, because participants viewed job security within the context of job performance, as a faculty member explained: "It seems to be the attitude of my colleagues and I, that we should earn our right to be employed each day—every day."

Not all faculty members agreed with these sentiments. Many felt anxious about their lack of employment security, which resulted in negative costs to faculty morale at two of the four institutions. Participants from these institutions explained that the low levels of faculty morale on their campus are a direct result of the increased administrative authority that imposes the restrictions. "Well, let's just say that most of us would not push [for a union] because we know what would happen. People have tried in the past and were fired . . . . Relating to the morale, right now it is pretty low." Another participant explained, "[Union] is something we do not use here. We have a term called faculty forum. You don't want to use those other types of label words. That is part of our culture." Another added, "We are not allowed to say union . . . . If you discuss it you can be fired."

Measuring job performance. The for-profit institutions represented in the study relied heavily on student evaluations and in-class peer evaluations to determine the performance levels of their faculty members. A full-time administrative faculty member explained, "I try to sit in on classes and talk to students in the hall during the breaks and get an idea of what's going on in the classroom." Student and faculty evaluations help to maintain quality, and also provide administrators with feedback regarding faculty members' classroom performance. The participating FPCUs made use of student evaluations to make decision's regarding a faculty member's future employment. A faculty member commented, "We look at what our students are saying about the facilitator." Another added,

> If we have indications in student evaluations that we have a specific problem, we may either run a quality assurance visit to take a look at the facilitator in the classroom, or we might go in and do some mentoring and try to correct some minor difficulties.

Although traditional institutions also utilize course evaluations to assess course quality and faculty success, evaluations often serve as a forum for students to make suggestions to faculty on how to improve the course. Conversely, faculty members at for-profit institutions whose student and/or peer evaluations are substandard either are placed on probationary status or are removed from the classroom. "If there are major difficulties then normally that faculty member is pulled off the line and is probably going to be placed in an 'observe' status . . ." Moreover, those who continually receive negative feedback from student evaluations risk losing their job. "If we get instructors that continually get negative feedback from students, then that's another quality assurance issue that we can use to determine that [name of university] is not for you."

Because student and peer evaluations are such valuable assessment tools, and because evaluations are based in part on whether a faculty member provides a level of service to their students, a perceived conflict of interest may exist. As on participant explained, "Somebody that has been here for ten years has to continue to perform [well] to remain employed. So, I think that affects how they interact in the classroom . . ." The assessment process coupled with the pressure to perform well places certain demands on a faculty member's activities with regard to student interactions.

Academic Constraints

Curricular decisions. Critics of for-profits point to the quality of the curriculum as a major weakness of FPCUs, specifically focusing on standardized curriculum. Generally speaking, FPCUs limit faculty members' authority over academic decisions for a number of reasons, but the level in which faculty are involved in developing their own courses and curriculum differs. It is a false assumption that all FPCUs standardize courses and curricula. Such notions are based on inaccurate observations that assume that all FPCUs behave in ways similar to the most visible institutions. As data show, FPCUs are not monoliths. Faculty members at two of the four institutions, for example, could design their own courses and choose their own textbooks; yet the administration and external advisory boards also played a major role in determining course content.

> The meaning in our program and the deliverables in our program are set by a focus group that is put together by the dean and the curriculum development team. And they put together a career path for the particular program that meets the needs of the employers for graduates.

Faculty members from FPCUs No. 1 and 2 do not have the option to design their own courses. Courses are standardized, and academic programs, although designed by faculty, are chosen by administrators, advisory groups, and the market. All four institutions seek to maintain standards to preserve the quality of their product—i.e., the quality of the students graduating from the institution. They make use of external parties to keep current with the needs of employers, a practice foreign to most traditional colleges and universities. Although one can argue that FPCUs that standardize curricula may not be serving students well, their motives are not without merit. For-profit institutions aspire to graduate high-quality students. Low-quality students lead to fewer enrollments, and without students, FPCUs would not be able to operate.

Corporate thinking assumes that academic quality is best maintained via standardization; standardization also creates efficiency. While this may be the case with certain organizations that produce products such as automobiles or hamburgers, education as a product is intangible and hard to define. Tension exists when definitions of quality differ. For instance, what one faculty member considers relevant knowledge another faculty member may consider inconsequential. On the one hand, the culture of academe asserts that faculty members should determine knowledge and content with regard to the courses they teach. FPCUs, on the other hand, must consider the delicate balance between maintaining quality while maximizing profit.

Practical knowledge. Faculty members at for-profit institutions approach teaching in a very different manner than faculty at the traditional institutions. Participants make certain that what they are teaching students is directly applicable to the needs of employers. Said differently, employers rather than faculty help to determine what students need to learn.

> From the business perspective, employers would like for [students] to be better prepared to communicate with others in their organization and others outside of the organization such as customers, clients, etc. So that gives us the focus on how [and] what direction we want to go educationally.

Participants spoke about how the focus on teaching practical skills calls for an approach to teaching that differs from traditional colleges and universities and is one way in which faculty autonomy is minimized. "Faculty must show a willingness to utilize [our] teaching and learning model." Faculty members that are unfamiliar or reluctant to learn the teaching methods FPCUs utilize will not succeed. For example, a faculty member whose prior teaching experience was at a traditional research institution was compelled by his students to modify his approach to teaching.

> On my midterm evaluations the students literally wrote "dumb it down, this is not the University of XXX," because they knew it's where I came from . . . . So I had to adjust and find middle ground. I realized they need

to face problems they see themselves. It is going to be the stuff that's going to help them in their career.

Modifying his teaching methods allowed his students to receive the kind of education they expected from the institution; yet at the same time faculty autonomy was compromised.

Exploring Faculty and Their Work

As this study has shown, faculty members at for-profit institutions live and work in environments that are both similar to and different from traditional nonprofit institutions. Faculty members who taught in degree programs at FPCUs had similar education and training to those of faculty who teach in comparable programs at private nonprofit and public institutions. Participants who taught in doctoral programs, for instance, held terminal degrees, and those who taught in two-year vocational programs held at least a bachelor's degree. Ironically, of the fifty-two participants in the study, only two received their educational training at an FPCU. The remainder attended traditional nonprofit institutions for at least one if not all of their degrees. In examining the nature of faculty work at FPCUs, three aspects stand out that help to differentiate faculty from traditional academe with those who work at for-profit institutions.

Faculty involvement in decision making. The most notable aspect of faculty work life at FPCUs is the lack of faculty autonomy. To those in traditional academe, the lack of autonomy can be viewed as an infringement on academic freedom. The notion of autonomy is connected to the idea that faculty members ought to be free to pursue "knowledge" without external hindrance. Since FPCUs do not concern themselves with knowledge production and research, then it follows that less faculty autonomy is warranted. Moreover, it is important to consider the amount of autonomy faculty members need when teaching in practically oriented programs such as welding and software design. This is not to say that faculty at FPCUs ought not to have the ability to decided what subject areas to cover in their courses. Instead, it may be better to examine the extent to which faculty autonomy exists within specific types of academic programs that may or may not warrant greater decision making authority by faculty.

Decision making at for-profit colleges and universities is shaped in many ways by corporate culture; decisions are made quickly, are data-driven, and reflect the needs of consumers. However, faculty members often are left out of the decision making process. Faculty engagement in the university community is minimized when faculty members are unable to participate in governing their institution. One can argue that many faculty members from traditional institutions are not heavily engaged in their university community and are more focused on their own endeavors. The major difference, however, is that faculty from traditional institutions can choose whether or not to be engaged. In the case of two participating institutions, increasing faculty involvement might improve morale, increase job satisfaction, and close the gap between the business and academic divisions of the institution.

Outputs and inputs are considered. For-profit institutions concern themselves more with student outputs rather than inputs. Traditional colleges and universities typically measure the academic characteristics of students before making admissions decisions. It is quite common for traditional universities to consider an individual's SAT or GRE scores and high school or undergraduate grade point average. Rather than focusing on standardized test scores and prior academic performance, for-profit institutions place a higher value on what their students have learned once they are in the classroom. Although admissions standards are admittedly weak, I am not arguing for more stringent admissions criteria at for-profits. Instead, my point is to identify a critical difference in the way students are evaluated.

Teaching and learning at for-profit institutions focuses on mastering core competencies that are predetermined for each course as well as for each degree program. Regardless of whether a faculty member can design his or her own course, measurable learning outcomes are the primary building block for creating a course. External constituencies such as employers are called upon to provide input to help determine the outcomes that will help shape the skills and abilities students need to be successful in the job market. In some cases, faculty members are required to cover predetermined content areas to assure that students receive a "fundamental" knowledge base; yet, it is important to point out that the aforementioned knowledge base is determined not only by faculty, but also by employers and the job market. In the current climate of accountability, traditional institutions would be well served to establish learning outcomes and place a greater focus on measuring whether students have met certain competencies. Calls for increased accountability in higher education may place traditional colleges and universities in a position where they may be forced to measure specific outcomes, without the option of determining what those outcomes are.

Unbundling of faculty roles and responsibilities. The manner in which for-profit institutions view the job responsibilities of their faculty provides insight into the educational paradigm that guides FPCUs. Faculty responsibilities are unbundled, meaning that teaching, writing curriculum, chairing dissertations, and administrative duties are separate activities, and faculty members are hired to perform specific tasks. Moreover, faculty can choose their work activities, whether developing a new course, teaching a class, sitting on a curriculum committee, or a combination of all three. Each task is a separate responsibility, and faculty members are compensated on a "per-task" basis.

As illustrated here, part-time faculty are primarily responsible for classroom teaching and on occasion may be contracted to help design a course. Full-time faculty members carry different responsibilities. In cases in which an FPCU primarily relies on part-time faculty to teach the majority of their courses, full-time faculty members are akin to administrators at traditional colleges and universities. Their major responsibilities lie outside the classroom: managing part-time faculty, hiring, firing, training, scheduling courses. At FPCUs that rely on similar numbers of part-time and full-time instructional faculty, full-time faculty will spend a great majority of their time in the classroom with limited administrative roles and responsibilities. There is no one mold from which to cast a part-time, let alone full-time, faculty member who works at a for-profit institution—a departure from traditional academe.

Conclusion

Not all for-profit institutions are alike. As this study shows, FPCUs share similarities but also have distinct features that make them unique. Part-time instructors make up over 90% of the instructional faculty at two of the institutions. Conversely, full-time faculty members constitute the majority of instructors at the remaining two. Some for-profit institutions focus primarily on graduate education, while others focus on education at or below the baccalaureate level. The types of degrees they offer typically indicate the types of faculty members they hire. Faculty members teaching at one institution may not qualify to each at another institution, because—unlike many traditional colleges and universities—academic degree programs are not similar across for-profit colleges and universities.

Faculty members' level of involvement in curriculum development also varies. Contrary to popular belief, many faculty members at FPCUs are allowed to design their own courses, although some are not. And when FPCUs standardize courses, they do so to ensure quality and consistency. One characteristic the institutions represented in the study share is a centralized decision making body. At all four institutions, the administration had final authority over most decisions, including those having to do with the types of courses and degree programs to offer.

In some respects, faculty roles at for-profit institutions bear a resemblance to faculty at traditional institutions. In large part, what determined the composition of faculty and the work modalities was the curriculum. Faculty who taught graduate classes were primarily individuals who held terminal degrees; those who taught baccalaureate classes uniformly held master's or doctoral degrees; certificate-based and vocational instructors parallel faculty that can be found at community colleges. Participation in curriculum development differed by institutional type and was influenced most by the administrative structure of the organization. Additionally, it was not uncommon for faculty at for-profit institutions to come from traditional higher education. Many of the participants who taught in master's and doctoral degree programs, for example, had retired from teaching and no longer desired a full-time job but were intrigued by the work at for-profits. Others came from business and industry, with at least a bachelor's degree, and enjoyed teaching a course. At institutions that relied on distance learning, many faculty seemed intrigued by the new technology and were eager to experiment.

One overlooked aspect of for-profit education is that the oft-commented convenience of courses extends not only to students, who are often working adults, but also to instructors. Many individuals who would like to teach a course are unable to do so when traditional campuses require them to be on campus. Of consequence, a ready labor force exists for for-profit teaching. Most of them are technically qualified to teach the types of courses needed at traditional colleges and universities.

For better or worse, for-profit colleges and universities have established themselves as viable alternatives to traditional private nonprofit and public institutions. Scholars in academe have begun to recognize the significant role these institutions are playing within the larger scope of higher education. We can no longer view for-profit postsecondary providers either as fringe institutions or monolithic organizations. To better understand their function and purpose, it will be important to distinguish one type from the other. As previously stated, not all for-profit colleges and universities are alike, nor are their faculty. This study offers unique insight into the specific elements and characteristics that comprise faculty composition and faculty work roles at four distinct types of for-profit institutions.

References

American Association of University Professors. (2001). Statement on government of colleges and universities. In *AAUP Policy Documents and Reports*, 9th ed. Washington, DC: AAUP.

American Association of University Professors. (2003). *Policy statement: Contingent appointments and the academic profession.* Retrieved November 24, 2003, from www.aaup.org/statements/SpchState/contingent.htm.

Austin, A. E. (1990). Faculty cultures, faculty values. *New Directions for Institutional Research, 17*(4), 61–74.

Becher, T. (1987). The disciplinary shaping of the profession. In B. R. Clark (Ed.), *The academic profession: National, disciplinary, and institutional settings* (pp. 271–303). Los Angeles: University of California Press.

Berg, G. A. (2004). *Lessons from the edge: For-profit and nontraditional higher education in America.* Westport, CT: Greenwood Publishing Group.

Carnegie Foundation for the Advancement of Teaching. (2006). Retrieved October 8, 2007, from www.carnegiefoundation.org/classifications/sub.asp?key=791.

Clark, B. R. (1983). *The higher education system: Academic organizations in cross-national perspective.* Los Angeles: University of California Press.

Education Commission of the States. (2000). *Report from the regions: Accreditors' perceptions of the role and impact of for-profit institutions in higher education* (Report No. PS-00-01W). Denver: Peter Ewell & Paula Schild.

Finkelstein, M. J. (1984). *The American academic profession.* Columbus: Ohio State University Press.

Gappa, J. M., & Leslie, D. W. (1993). *The invisible faculty: Improving the status of part-timers in higher education.* San Francisco: Jossey-Bass.

Jacobs, F. (1998). Using part-time faculty more effectively. In D. W. Leslie (Ed.), *The growing use of part-time faculty: Understanding causes and effects.* New Directions for Higher Education, *104,* 81–88. San Francisco: Jossey-Bass.

Kerr, C. (2001). *The uses of the university,* 5th ed. Cambridge, MA: Harvard University Press.

Kinser, K. (2006). From main street to wall street: For-profit higher education. *ASHE Higher Education Report, 31*(5). San Francisco: Jossey-Bass.

Kirp, D. L. (2004). *Shakespeare, Einstein, and the bottom line: The marketing of higher education.* Cambridge, MA: Harvard University Press.

Lechuga, V. M. (2006). *The changing landscape of the academic profession: The culture of faculty at for-profit colleges and universities.* New York: Routledge.

National Center for Education Statistics. (1998). *Faculty staff in postsecondary institutions.* Washington, DC: U.S. Department of Education.

National Center for Education Statistics. (2003). *Enrollment in postsecondary institutions, Fall 2001 and financial statistics, fiscal year 2001.* Washington, DC: U.S. Department of Education.

Pusser, B., & Turner, S. T. (2004). Non-profit and for-profit governance in higher education. In R.G. Ehrenberg (Ed.), *Governing academia* (pp. 235–257). Ithaca, NY: Cornell University Press.

Rudolph, F. (1990). *The American college and university: A history.* Athens: The University of Georgia Press.

Schuster, J. H., & Finkelstein, M. J. (2006). *The American faculty: The restructuring of academic work and careers.* Baltimore: Johns Hopkins University Press.

Strauss, A. L., & Corbin, J. M. (1990). *Basics of qualitative research: Grounded theory procedures and techniques.* Newbury Park, CA: Sage Publications.

Tierney, W. G., & Hentschke, G. C. (2007). *New players, different game: Understanding the rise of for-profit colleges and universities.* Baltimore: Johns Hopkins University Press.

Tierney, W. G., & Rhoads, R. A. (1993). *Faculty socialization as cultural process: A mirror of institutional commitment.* ASHE-ERIC Higher Education Report No. 93-6. Washington, DC: The George Washington University, School of Education and Human Development.

Washburn, J. (2005). *University Inc.: The corporate corruption of American higher education.* New York: Basic Books.

4

DIFFERENCES IN ACADEMIC WORK AT TRADITIONAL AND FOR-PROFIT POSTSECONDARY INSTITUTIONS

Policy Implications for Academic Freedom

William G. Tierney and Vicente M. Lechuga

erhaps no single principle has been as important to higher education over the last century as academic freedom. It is the fundamental precept that promotes open discourse and allows for the free exchange of ideas on college and university campuses. The Supreme Court has stated that academic freedom is necessary for the health and welfare not only of academe but also of a democratic society. As John Dewey (1936) wrote, "Since freedom of mind and freedom of expression are at the root of all freedom, to deny freedom in education is a crime against democracy" (p. 6). Academic freedom also suggests a stance for a postsecondary institution. Individuals within the academy are expected to be able to debate issues with one another and in the larger society without fear of recrimination or loss of employment. Although most members of the academic community endorse the tenets of academic freedom, disagreements about how such policies should be interpreted and applied are more intense than ever at traditional colleges and universities (TCUs).

One relatively new area where academic freedom is contested is in the for-profit higher education sector. Recent incidents have shed light on the significance that for-profit colleges and universities (FPCUs), such as the University of Phoenix, place on academic freedom, and raise a question whether FPCUs should be considered within the universe of post-secondary institutions or something different yet again. That is, if academic freedom is a fundamental precept for a postsecondary institution, then what does it mean when an institution does not share that belief? The question is more than merely an intellectual puzzle, for its answer goes to the heart of what society should expect of postsecondary institutions in the twenty-first century.

Academic freedom and for-profit institutions might be considered terms in contradiction. On the one hand, one may argue that for-profit degree-granting colleges and universities substantiate the argument that certain institutions can operate without the need for academic freedom. For-profit institutions are first and foremost profit-seeking entities whose primary functions are twofold: (1) to provide students with the necessary skill sets to succeed in the current job market and (2) to generate a profit. From this perspective, academic freedom is either unnecessary or infringes on the ability of for-profits to conduct business. On the other hand, some will suggest that policies that limit academic freedom in and outside of the classroom only serve to weaken the system of higher education. To paraphrase John Dewey when he became the American Association of University Professors' (AAUP) first president—to infringe upon academic freedom in one classroom is to threaten academic freedom in all classrooms.

In what follows, we explore the notion of academic freedom and consider how it frames faculty work in traditional institutions. We then consider what drives faculty work in for-profits. We suggest that academic freedom in for-profit institutions is of peripheral concern, which places the institution in a fundamentally different stance with regard to the public than that of non-profit public and private institutions. To substantiate the position we provide data pertaining to academic freedom in the for-profit sector. In doing so, we also argue that academic freedom encourages healthy discourse surrounding controversial issues, and its absence only serves to curtail thoughtful discussion. We examine what the implications are for the academy and suggest that protecting academic freedom benefits the public by creating an environment that fosters participation in a democratic society.

Faculty Work at Traditional Institutions: Academic Freedom Drives Faculty Work

Although there may be any number of starting points for determining how faculty roles have been configured in American higher education, the most pertinent place to begin is in the late nineteenth century. Faculty who had been trained in Europe, primarily in Germany and England, returned to the United States with the idea that faculty work should be more than teaching. Philanthropists had the income to support such a desire. Thus, by the start of the twentieth century, a handful of colonial institutions and church-related colleges had experienced dramatic institutional makeovers, and new-comers had entered the academic ranks such as Stanford, Duke, Vanderbilt, Cornell, and Chicago. In 1900 the Association of American Universities (AAU) was created and laid claim to institutional greatness for American research universities, not simply in the United States, but throughout the world.

Concomitantly, previously undeveloped areas of knowledge and inquiry began to become professionalized. By 1920, professional associations existed, for example, in political science, economics, anthropology, and history. Reports such as those written by Abraham Flexner in 1910 on medical train-ing or the work of Elwood Cubberly in education sought to give intellectual rigor and shape to professional fields. The result was that academic standards came into existence and expectations of the faculty rose. Whereas in the early nineteenth century a typical professor may well have been a minister who sought to imbue his charges with a sense of devotion and moral training, the new American institution required that faculty have some sort of scientific training to impart to graduate and undergraduate students. Rather than rely on Europe for that training, the United States sought to develop institutions at home that could prepare faculty.

The growth of American higher education and the professionalization of the faculty had many results that few could have predicted. Prior to the twen-tieth century, administration at a college meant a president and perhaps a registrar and dean of students. The president hired and fired faculty at will. A board of trustees, rather than the faculty, held the trust for the direction of the organization. Faculty meetings, if they existed, concerned the grading and evaluation of students. Faculty had no input on budgets, buildings, or the nature of their own work. The faculty had one role—to teach undergrad-uate students. Although most professors taught full-time, their work was not that different from other mid-level individuals in a professional job. Just as individuals who work in a store are valued for their labor but are not direc-tors of their work, professors were valued for their teaching but were little more than hired hands, albeit in a somewhat refined workplace.

By the early years of the twentieth century, however, the size of the faculty had more than doubled. As institutions grew, the size of the administration increased as well. Faculty returned from Europe with a desire for greater autonomy in their professional lives. The Germanic concept of *Lehrfreiheit* came with graduate student training in the disciplines, and American students learned their lessons well. The concept pertained to "the right of the university professor to freedom of inquiry and to freedom of teaching, the right to study and to report on his findings in an atmosphere of consent" (Rudolph, 1962, p. 412). The desire for freedom of inquiry and teaching and the rise of professional associations was on a collision course with the manner in which colleges and universities were run. Faculty no longer saw themselves as the equivalent of hired labor, but they had not yet determined what their new role would be. Conflict was bound to ensue.

Lehrfreiheit became the forerunner of the American ideal of academic freedom. The violations of a professor's academic freedom from that period are legendary and well documented. Richard Ely, for example, a liberal economist at the University of Wisconsin, lost his job in 1894 because of his support for labor unions (Schrecker, 1983, p. 27). Scott Nearing was fired in 1915 from the University of Pennsylvania because he opposed the use of child labor in coal mines (Slaughter, 1980, p. 52). John Mecklin, an outspoken liberal professor at Lafayette College was forced to resign in 1913 because of his philosophical relativism, interest in pragmatism, and teaching of evolution (Metzger, 1955, p. 201). In perhaps the most infamous case during that time, Edward Ross of Stanford University used what today would be considered hate speech to argue for the rights of unions and to warn of the threat of imported labor. Mrs. Stanford, the sole trustee of the university, demanded that President Jordan fire Ross. He lost his job in 1900 (Tierney, 2004).

In addition to the creation of disciplinary associations as a means to confront issues related to the infringement of academic freedom, faculty formed an association in 1915 that cut across disciplines and demanded professional rights. The American Association of University Professors (AAUP) chose John Dewey as its first president. During its first two years, the AAUP investigated over thirty cases of infringements on academic freedom. They established a committee to conduct investigations and set about developing policies that protected academic freedom.

The result of these actions was fourfold. First, academic freedom became enshrined as a hallmark declaration for American higher education. In declaring that institutions of higher education were conducted for the common good, individuals agreed that the search for truth and its free exposition were essential. Second, to preserve academic freedom, a system of tenure came into existence that guaranteed faculty lifetime employment and protected them from being fired at will if they studied a topic that drew the ire of administrators or legislators. Third, in order for academic freedom to remain a hallmark of the institution, the concept of shared governance came into existence. Shared governance acknowledges the central role of the faculty in governing the internal affairs of the institution such as the hiring, evaluation, and firing of faculty, the standards for admitting students, and the curricula. And fourth, the role of faculty changed. Research, teaching, and service became the three primary functions of academic work. The assumption was that to be good teachers, the vast majority of professors needed to participate in research; for some faculty, research would be their primary activity. If shared governance was essential, then service to the institution and the profession was also necessary.

Although such a transformation did not occur overnight, by the end of World War II, the vast majority of traditional colleges and universities more or less accepted these basic precepts. Many individuals complained about one or another aspect—especially tenure policies. But they also recognized that after tenure came into existence, shared governance became the norm, and America emerged as a global superpower, American higher education became the envy of the world.

This brief overview of academic freedom and faculty work in traditional organizations is obviously an idealized type. A handful of postsecondary institutions, for example, do not have tenure. At many institutions, research is far less important than teaching. Although tenure remains a basic precept, the reality is that more part-time and non–tenure-track professors are hired today than full-time tenure-track faculty (Benjamin, 2003). Similarly, shared governance is still said to be important and valued, but administrators have greater authority on campus today than a generation ago. Nevertheless, the modalities remain in place and stand in contrast to the norms and policies at for-profit colleges and universities.

Faculty Work at For-Profit Institutions: Curricula Drive Faculty Work

One may ask why it is necessary to understand academic freedom, and how it relates to the role of faculty in traditional organizations to discuss faculty at for-profit institutions. We do so because in one sense, the contrast is not very significant, and yet in another, the differences are vast. That is, at most traditional and for-profit institutions, faculty teach courses to students. However, to make such a facile comparison is, as previously stated, a bit like implying that since a bicycle and an airplane are both means of transportation, they are quite similar. As we previously outlined, although faculty teach classes at traditional institutions, the impetus of the organization is quite different from a simple desire to offer courses, much less to make a profit.

In some respects, traditional colleges and universities have been arranged more to serve the needs of the faculty than to meet the needs of other constituencies. Some will argue that such a statement makes self-evident the criticism that traditional institutions ill serve their various constituencies. We disagree. Traditional colleges and universities have had as their priority a concern for academic freedom and the search for truth. The assumption has been that such a search is not a self-encapsulated benefit to those who do the searching—the faculty. The argument has instead been made (and supported by the Supreme Court) that society gains when faculty are provided with the conditions for the unfettered search for truth. If tenure is nothing more than lifetime employment, then it is merely a sinecure for intellectuals. However, tenure came about to ensure academic freedom, and that protection has been supported time and again in the courts and in public opinion polls.

As we have noted, such a statement appeals to an ideal type with regard to organizational purpose. Clearly, not all faculty lay claim to searching for truth every time they set foot in a classroom or research setting. The same may be said, however, about any overarching ideology. During the course of their lives, not all of America's citizens will need to call upon the First Amendment to support what they wish to express. Every time an individual opens his or her mouth, it is not a test of free speech. However, the ideology helps frame how people define themselves as citizens of the United States. We suggest that the same may be said for faculty at traditional colleges and universities. In what follows, however, we point out that at for-profit colleges and universities, rather than a devotion to academic freedom, what determines academic work and faculty work is quite another goal altogether.

One way to think about for-profit colleges and universities is with regard to their fiscal status. Some are publicly traded entities that are set up as corporations where shareholders own a portion of the company. Others are privately held companies where an investor, or group of investors, owns the institution. While the fiscal implications for profit sharing, ownership, strategic direction, and manner of corporate decision making are important, whether an institution is a publicly traded or privately held company does not appear to influence significantly the makeup, modalities, or work of the faculty.

Instead, what in large part determines faculty work and modalities are what we define as five curricular categories. The functional categories pertain not only to what is taught, but also to the structural frameworks employed to define and deliver courses. In turn, these categories impact the expectations of professional and regional accreditation associations that also frame faculty work. We suggest, then, that just as a desire for academic freedom determined how faculty work was constructed at traditional institutions, the curriculum determines academic work at proprietary institutions. Thus, policies pertaining to academic freedom take on an entirely different meaning. An overview of the curricular categories is in order.

Vocational Curricula

The most common type of for-profit colleges in the United States is the less-than-two-year, non–degree-granting institution (National Center for Education Statistics [NCES], 2001). This type of college enrolls the largest proportion of students attending for-profit institutions. Such institutions offer a curriculum that traditionally has been associated with for-profit education. Fashion design colleges, court reporting schools, trade schools for computer technicians and administrative assistants, and other similar programs are examples of standalone proprietary institutions that offer training usually in one or two locations. The courses are generally not applicable toward a degree; upon completion, the student receives a diploma that enables him or her to apply for work in a particular trade.

Bryman College, for example, offers programs in medical office management, massage therapy, and business administrative assistance. Students are provided with an education that emphasizes practical skills that lead to employment in a vocational area. Like many for-profit institutions that offer vocational training, Bryman is nationally accredited. National accrediting agencies such as the Accrediting Commission of Career Schools and Colleges (ACCSC), the Accrediting Council for Independent Colleges and Schools (ACICS), and the Accrediting Council for Continuing Education and Training (ACCET) provide national accreditation to career colleges across the country.

Certificate Curricula

As employers seek out individuals whose skill competencies are independently certified, for-profit institutions are catering to this new student market by offering courses that lead to certification. Certificate courses generally fall within two types: additional courses that are added to diploma programs to meet minimum standards set forth by a specific organization or agency, and standalone "course sets" that a student must complete to qualify for a specific job. The central difference between vocational and certificate curricula pertain to the certification of competencies by an independent group. Vocational curricula are courses that provide students with fundamental skills that are required for a given vocation. An administrative assistant program, for example, may provide students with basic clerical skills such as word processing, basic accounting, and Internet proficiency. When the student has completed the training, he or she qualifies for an entry-level position as an office assistant.

Although they prepare students for industry certification, for-profit colleges and universities do not directly offer IT certification, for example. These providers "operate outside Title IV of the Higher Education Amendments and the Integrated Postsecondary Education Data System (IPEDS). That is, they do not participate in the federal student aid and reporting systems. We thus know little about their students" (Adelman, 2000, pp. 24–25). The primary vendors, such as Microsoft, Novell, and Cisco, as well as industry associations, establish the certification criteria.

Undergraduate Curricula

A third form of curricula offering pertains to coursework that leads to an associate or bachelor's degree. As we have discussed, most degrees offered by for-profits are practical majors that lead to specific jobs such as in business or engineering. While an institution may offer general education requirements and a few electives, the central focus of the curriculum is on a specific number of established courses that a student must take to receive a professional degree.

Graduate Curricula

Although master's and doctor's degrees are the least common curricula to be offered by proprietary institutions, they also are seen as an area with tremendous growth potential. As with undergraduate curricula, the focus is on degrees that are more professional in nature and that do not require extensive laboratory work or primary research. Thus, one is likely to see coursework leading to a master's degree or doctorate in education, nursing, or business, but not in areas such as medicine, biochemistry, or physics.

Curricula Structures and Delivery Mechanisms

The final category, which has significant implications for faculty work, is how FPCUs arrange their courses and programs. One commonality among traditional institutions is the structural nature of what is meant by a "course." A "course" is a discrete body of knowledge that a faculty member develops and offers over a set period of time for a specific number of units. When courses are combined with one another, they count toward a major and a degree; when a predetermined number of credits have been accumulated, the student receives a degree. Programs are made up of specified sets of courses. Programs of study can lead to majors, degrees, and other certifications upon successful completion of the set of courses.

Although some for-profit institutions mirror traditional notions of the structure of curricula and how a course should be delivered, there is also significant variation. Credit for work experience is much more common at for-profit institutions. Courses frequently begin and end irrespective of the start of a fall or spring semester or quarter. The mastery of a skill set, especially in certification courses, is much more important than the accumulation of credits. Students are more likely to utilize the Internet and Web-based learning than at traditional institutions. Indeed, the manner of delivery is a key decision at for-profit institutions, whereas at traditional institutions, delivery is more a matter of matching specific instructors with particular courses at predetermined times.

Profiling the Faculty at For-Profits

The hiring policies for faculty at for-profit institutions are designed in response to the demands by associations that were formed according to what constitutes "faculty work" at traditional organizations. That is, traditional colleges and universities framed faculty life as a way to ensure that academic freedom existed. To guarantee this freedom, faculty were given considerable autonomy in their teaching and research; service to the profession and organization was also deemed important. Tenure and full-time status for faculty were assumed to be essential. Such assumptions, however, create inevitable tension for an organization that does not organize its activities around the same beliefs. Rather than preserve academic freedom, for-profit organizations seek to provide effective curricula in efficient time formats in order to turn a profit. The result is that what constitutes faculty work and who populates the role of the professorate differ dramatically from traditional institutions as illustrated in Chapter 3.

In some respects, due to accreditation requirements, those who populate faculty roles at FPCUs bear a resemblance to faculty at traditional institutions. Faculty who teach graduate classes are primarily individuals who hold terminal degrees; those who teach baccalaureate classes uniformly hold master's or doctoral degrees; and certificate-based and vocational instructors parallel faculty one might find at community colleges. Indeed, it is not uncommon for faculty at FPCUs to come from traditional higher education. Many of them who teach in bachelor's or master's degree programs, for example, have retired from teaching and no longer desire a full-time job, but are intrigued by the work of for-profits.

Some professors are the equivalent of "freeway flyers"; they teach multiple classes at numerous institutions. As stated in the previous chapters, others come from business and industry, with at least a bachelor's degree, and enjoy teaching a course. At institutions that rely on distance learning, many faculty are intrigued by the new technology and are eager to experiment. One overlooked aspect of for-profit education is that the oft-commented convenience of courses extends not only to students, who are often working adults, but also to instructors. Many individuals who would like to teach a course are unable to do so when or where traditional campuses require. Consequently, a ready labor force exists for for-profit teaching. Most of them are technically qualified to teach the types of courses needed compared to TCUs.

An anomaly exists inasmuch as for-profit faculty are generally a bit older than their confreres at traditional institutions; they are also more diverse in terms of race and gender. That is, one might assume that if faculty are older, there would be more white men teaching classes. However, the reverse is the case. While a significant percentage of faculty come from the ranks of retirees with time on their hands, a similarly large number of faculty are concurrently employed in business and industry. Simply stated, the pool of women and people of color to choose from in business and industry is larger than in the elite graduate programs that offer Ph.D.s. The programs that for-profits offer also have larger numbers of people of color in them than the panoply of departments that require staffing at traditional institutions. There are more people of color and women, for example, in nursing, education, and business than in biochemistry, electrical engineering, and classics.

As noted, one impetus for higher education change at the turn of the twentieth century was the faculty themselves. The pattern had been to hire full-time tenure-track staff, some of whom had returned from their European education with a desire to conduct research and to have greater say in the affairs of the institution. At for-profit institutions, the pattern has been, in large part, not to hire full-time tenure-track faculty. Research also has never been a component for academic work at FPCUs, while relevant successful employment and experience has been a major component.

To be sure, some variation exists with regard to hiring patterns at FPCUs, although tenure is rare. (Tenure exists, for example, in several FPCU law schools.) At some institutions, such as DeVry University, about half of the faculty are full-time. Other institutions such as the University of Phoenix, have what appear to be a number of full-time faculty, but they spend "the majority of their time doing administrative tasks" (Floyd, 2005). Vocational institutions also may have full-time instructors, but they parallel their counterparts in a community college, albeit without tenure. A very few institutions also have long-term contracts, and the faculty at these institutions, such as Argosy University, claim that they have a great deal of input into the direction of the curriculum (Berg, 2005, p. 225). The bottom line is that for-profits want their faculty to teach, and their assumption is that tenure is at best unnecessary, and at worst a serious impediment, for achieving the goals of the organization.

FPCUs may want their faculty to teach, but given accreditation requirements, they also recognize that faculty must be involved in the governance of the organization in some manner. It is not uncommon, for example, that a visiting accreditation team might comment that a for-profit college "exhibits a lack of mature faculty integration or a common faculty appreciation of the proper role of faculty governance. While faculty members have individual roles, as a whole, they lack a sense of a collective role." Such a statement highlights an inevitable tension. Members of accreditation teams overwhelmingly come from the ranks of traditional institutions. The idea of shared governance in business is a bizarre concept for those who work in companies whose purpose is to turn a profit. True, a miniscule percentage of organizations are actually "worker-run" or "worker-owned," but the paradigm in place is one that rejects the idea of shared governance. Although hierarchical and linear decision making may be out of fashion, no one makes a serious argument that business and industry need to adopt the model that exists at traditional colleges and universities. Furthermore, with many employees owning shares of their FPCUs, corporate accountability to shareholders has no analogue in TCUs.

As a result, FPCUs face criticism from accrediting agencies for their lack of shared governance. Furthermore, when employees are part-timers, it is no easy task to incorporate them into a decision making framework, especially when many are also employed elsewhere and seek part-time teaching for its prestige, fulfillment, or additional income. Indeed, traditional colleges and universities face the same conundrum. While standing governance committees already exist at postsecondary institutions, most of them do not accommodate part-time workers; as the percentage of part-time employees increases, colleges and universities struggle with how to incorporate part-timers into governance.

However, at FPCUs, the challenge is even more severe because frequently no governance structure exists for faculty. If we consider why shared governance arose in the first place, we can appreciate why it is so weak at for-profits. Shared governance, like tenure, came about to protect academic freedom. If academic freedom is not of concern at an institution, then why are cumbersome decision making and employment structures necessary? The answer from those who work at FPCUs is that such structures impede their effectiveness. The answer from those who work at traditional institutions is that academic freedom is essential, and that profit ought not to be the overriding motive for offering a postsecondary education. Notice that each argument can be true and does not directly or completely address the other.

Academic Freedom at For-Profits

We have written elsewhere about the challenges to academic freedom that have taken place at traditional colleges and universities (Tierney & Lechuga, 2005). The Ward Churchill controversy, the firing and subsequent trial of Sami Al-Arian at the University of South Florida, and the more recent events surrounding the creation of an "enemies list" of "the dirty thirty" (Makdisi, 2006) liberal professors at UCLA point out that challenges to academic freedom are still common in academe. However, when such challenges occur, the norm is that there is a great deal of public discourse and debate. Numerous individuals argue, often quite passionately, about the issue or people who are being attacked. Underpinning these discussions is the assumption that public engagement is a vital role of postsecondary institution. Again, such an assumption is predicated on a belief pertaining to academic freedom.

In what follows we offer some examples of infringements on academic freedom at for-profit colleges and universities. The point of these examples is to contrast and highlight the different stances taken by FPCUs and TCUs. The examples underscore an implied set of policies pertaining to academic freedom that deviate from the norms of traditional academia.

The Perils of Blogging

In December 2005, Meg Spohn, a faculty member and head of the Communications and Composition Department at DeVry University in Westminster, Colorado, was called into her dean's office and promptly fired. Her dean did not specify why the university had decided to terminate her employment other than to state that DeVry became aware of her personal Web site, alleging that she had made derogatory statements about the university and its students (Harsanyl, 2005). Spohn, a Ph.D. candidate at the University of Denver who also holds a master's degree from Harvard University, frequently posts her thoughts on her Web log, or blog—an online forum that serves as a personal journal.

Spohn discusses on her blog a variety of subjects ranging from her travels through Yugoslavia to her thoughts on feminism. Her job at DeVry University also was a topic of dialogue. Spohn posted comments about the institution's practice of hiring faculty members who were practitioners from the field rather than individuals with teaching backgrounds, and about the time-consuming online training she was required to complete. After she was informed of her dismissal, Spohn was escorted to her office to pack her belongings and then to her car, without anyone knowing she had been released: "I was not allowed to say goodbye to anybody or talk to anyone on the way out, ostensibly for the purpose of 'confidentiality.' I was hustled out of there in a surprisingly furtive fashion. Nobody even knew I was gone" (M. Spohn, personal communication, December 16, 2005).

What is unsettling about this incident is the notion that a faculty member can be dismissed without warning or due process for apparently espousing an opinion. DeVry did not dismiss Spohn for her incompetence;

she was fired because she held an unpopular opinion. Moreover, that a faculty member can be dismissed without knowing the nature of their offending remarks is troubling. On her Web log, Spohn writes:

> [There was] no warning, disciplinary procedure, discussion, or any other process by which I was notified of the "problem." This was especially egregious, as previous instances of faculty having "objectionable" postings on their blogs have been treated by discussing it with the faculty member. I was fired outright without any opportunity for discussion at all. (M. Spohn, personal communication, December 16, 2005)

While DeVry University did not violate any laws, given that Colorado upholds an "at-will" employment doctrine and the institution is a private enterprise, it is important not to overlook the fact that the university operates within the higher education landscape. Stated differently, DeVry, like most for-profit institutions, is both part of the proprietary sector of business and industry and part of the higher education community. Each community upholds a specific set of values that are reflected in the practices and policies that govern the institution. It is at the intersection of these values that academic freedom is contested.

Butts in Seats

In January of 2005, the television news magazine *60 Minutes* ran a story that detailed allegations of fraud at several campuses owned by Career Education Corporation (CEC), one of the largest for-profit higher education corporations in the country. Students who were interviewed stated that the college they attended boasted a 98 percent job placement and only later discovered those claims to be false. Upon graduating with a degree in fashion, the students that were interviewed were unable to find full-time employment in the industry. Instead, they were employed on a part-time hourly basis in retail selling T-shirts. Admissions officers, who spoke anonymously, explained that their job was little more than sales. Said one: "We're selling you that you're gonna have a 95 percent chance that you are gonna have a job paying $35,000 to $40,000 a year by the time they are done in 18 months. We later found out it's not true at all" (Fager, 2005). The culture of organization, said the individual, "was all about the numbers. Getting students enrolled, getting students in the seats. Keeping students in the seats, getting them passed enough to graduate, and then trying to get them any job we could." (Fager, 2005). It is important to note that all of the CEC employees who had been interviewed for the *60 Minutes* segment were *former* employees; no current employees were willing to publicly comment, and faced dismissal if they did.

During the 1980s, for-profit higher institutions were under scrutiny by Congress. Proprietary colleges were seen as fly-by-night institutions that defrauded the federal government out of hundreds of millions of financial aid dollars. The interviews reflected what many had claimed continued to take place at for-profit institutions. Moreover, a report by the U.S. Department of Education alleged that the University of Phoenix was involved in similar devious acts. Salaries of University of Phoenix admissions officers were based on recruitment and enrollment figures. Individuals with high enrollment figures received significant raises, free trips, bonuses, and awards—a direct violation of Sections 487 (a) and 487 (a) (20) of the Higher Education Act (U.S. Department of Education, 2003, p. 27). The report also stated "72 percent of the recruiters interviewed stated that it was always about the numbers—all about 'butts in seats' or 'asses in classes'—to use the vernacular commonly heard at UOP" (Blumenstyk, 2004, p. 3). Admissions officers who failed to meet their quota received little or no pay raise and were in danger of losing their jobs.

The response by the for-profit higher education sector to the *60 Minutes* story reflected a primary concern for revenue generation. The day after the exposé, Merrill Lynch (2005) issued a report that focused on the financial ramifications of the story. "While the piece is clearly negative it does remove the overhang of what was always expected to be a negative report, and we believe that some of the impact was already built into the stocks which were down on Friday in anticipation of the piece airing this weekend. . . . We would expect that the stocks in the sector could come under further pressure as a result of the program" (Merrill Lynch, 2005, p. 1). Moreover, the Merrill Lynch report (2005), in a section headed *Political Risk*, stated "Another potential concern is any potential political risk related to the piece. . . . This is a particularly important time as the Higher Education Act is up for reauthorization. However, the political environment is more favorable for for-profit institutions than it has been in the past."

On the same day the *60 Minutes* piece aired, Career Education Corporation (CEC) released a statement; however, the press release failed to address any of the allegations made in the story. It merely stated that CEC had "built our reputation through adhering to good business practices, setting clear values and acting with integrity . . . our success cannot be maintained in any manner other than through a strict focus on integrity and quality" (Career Education Corporation, press release, January 30, 2005).

We attempted to contact faculty members from several CEC campuses to inquire whether the story that aired was accurate in its depiction of CEC and the for-profit higher education sector, but we encountered several barriers in the process. To begin, it was not possible to obtain any information about faculty members who taught for the Career Education Corporation. CEC campuses did not list information about their faculty on institutional Web sites. We subsequently placed several phone calls to a number of CEC campuses to solicit contact information for faculty members. After speaking with several CEC administrators, only two of the eight institutions we contacted returned our calls. The remaining institutions were unwilling to speak with us even though we guaranteed anonymity to their faculty.

One of the two CEC faculty members who agreed to be interviewed was quite candid with regard to the *60 Minutes* story and Career Education Corporation in general. He mentioned that CEC monitors faculty members' phone calls and e-mails, and asked that we contact him using his cell phone. He explained that he had been a faculty member and administrator at several community colleges before moving into the for-profit higher education sector. He described CEC as "a very autocratic organization" that lacked academic freedom. During our brief conversation he revealed why he chose to speak to us: "I'm interviewing and I'll probably be out in a couple of months. I'll be glad when I'm out of here. I've had enough." The other faculty member who had initially agreed to speak to us ultimately declined, stating, "I am not sure we can do this. I'll get back to you." He did not return our calls.

Research Barriers

In previous work, we found other for-profit institutions to be equally reticent to participate in our research efforts. For example, we recently conducted a study pertaining to faculty work life at for-profit degree-granting institutions and encountered similar barriers. Potential participants were informed that the purpose of the study was to understand the roles and responsibilities of faculty members at for-profit colleges and universities. Participants were guaranteed confidentiality and had the option to withdraw from participation at a later date if they changed their minds. After soliciting several faculty participants using e-mail addresses found on one institution's public Web directory, several faculty members agreed to participate. However, the dean of academic affairs of this institution forwarded an e-mail to all faculty members who taught at several branch campuses stating:

> We should not respond to such inquiries without OBT legal and PR's approval. Debbie G. coordinates this kind of approval process. This person is directly contacting lots of our faculty at the three campuses. The proper protocol . . . is to get permission from the organization's leadership first. [Author] has not done so, consequently his request should be viewed as being bogus. Officials [from his institution] have been notified of this breach in research protocol. (Lechuga, 2006, p. 157)

Faculty members from other institutions that participated in this study revealed several concerns related to infringements on their ability to speak out. This was especially true when it came to the notion of addressing unfavorable work environments. At one institution, we inquired whether faculty had considered forming a union to address these issues. Said one respondent, "I do not want to answer that because other people can hear my answer. We are not in a private office . . . faculty do not have private offices" (Lechuga, 2006, p. 147). She later explained that the culture of the institution was one that looked quite unfavorably on unions. Another participant added, "We are not allowed to say union . . . . If you discuss it you can be fired" (p. 185). The university was aware of such issues and attempted to respond to them; however, their attempts seemed disingenuous at best. After being notified that she was on a committee that was tasked with examining faculty members' concerns over poor working conditions, one participant remarked, "The day I saw I was on that committee I said, 'I have to start looking for a job, because I'm going to get fired'" (p. 147).

The previous quotes reveal how faculty members at for-profit institutions are constrained in their ability to speak out for fear of losing their job. This type of environment can prohibit frank dialogue with members of an institution's administration regarding ways to improve such things as curricula, personnel, student quality, and other facets of the institution. Furthermore, the nature of the relationship between FPCU administrators and the faculty members reveals the constraints associated with a work environment that limits a faculty members' academic freedom.

Considering the Differences in Faculty Work

We have demonstrated here the differences in expectations of faculty roles and work between traditional and for-profit institutions and why these differences have developed. Although both sectors deliver a similar curricular "product," what they expect from their "providers"—the faculty—is significantly different. From a traditionalist perspective, what the for-profits are doing is a violation of true academic life, and hence, a bastardization of the role of the faculty. The response from the FPCUs is that they are doing something quite different from traditional institutions; given their different purposes and markets, they should not be compared directly with TCUs. Indeed, critics of the traditional sector would suggest that many TCU faculty roles have become moribund and risk-averse. For-profit institutions develop a business plan with the risk built in. They assume little risk from the faculty, because they do not think of academic freedom and its accoutrements (tenure, shared governance, research, and service) as necessary for what they are attempting to do.

We have heard it said that when the film industry began, innovators such as Charlie Chaplin were a veritable one-man show: Chaplin wrote, produced, directed, and starred in his movies. Today, of course, the film industry has distinct individuals who write, produce, direct, and star in movies. It is rare indeed when an individual assumes more than one role in the development of a movie. The analogy is then made to teaching. At traditional institutions, both then and now, one finds the equivalent of multiple Charlie Chaplins. Faculty do everything—develop the syllabus, determine when and where they will teach, decide who their students will be, and star in the show. The response by those at traditional institutions is that such an analogy is not apt. They argue that what is really intended by such analogies is for the capitalists at for-profits (and elsewhere) to claim the intellectual property of faculty and to reduce professors to little more than day laborers.

As the demand and supply of postsecondary education increase, possibilities of peaceful coexistence between FPCUs and TCUs may erode. Those at FPCUs are quite critical of ideas such as tenure and shared governance. Those at traditional colleges and universities find equally repugnant the notion that profit has replaced core values such as academic freedom with policies designed to increase revenue production. TCUs are comfortable with moderate, sustainable change, and FPCUs are fomenting disruptive technologies. Alternatively, we may be seeing the distinctions that occur when for-profit organizations produce services heretofore produced by public and nonprofit organizations.

Obviously, no one can predict the future with certainty. However, in a system as vast as postsecondary education in the United States, we wish to offer a question. It appears self-evident that the postsecondary "industry" has two quite different notions of the role of faculty, just as one group accepts the notion of capitalism (being in business to make a profit) and the other views profit making in education with suspicion. Similarly, the idea that either traditional or for-profit institutions are going to go away seems far-fetched. One is a mature industry that undoubtedly will undergo transformation but that is likely to remain more similar to what it is today than different. The other is a growth industry that similarly will undergo changes, but the demand for their "product" exists and will not lessen in an age in which knowledge and information are essential. Why, then, is it not possible for both sectors to define more clearly the policies that delineate how they operate, and, of consequence, what they expect of faculty?

It is difficult to imagine that all of postsecondary education in the United States will adopt the for-profit faculty model. If academic freedom as a central precept were eliminated from all of postsecondary education, then the country would suffer in numerous ways—classroom dialogue would be cheapened, research would be circumscribed, and the country would lose a vital link to that which it holds essential: free speech. However, it seems a very weak argument indeed to say that FPCUs, who claim a different undertaking, must adhere to the same policies, beliefs, and strategies of traditional institutions. Some might argue that a professor in a for-profit classroom should enjoy the same right of academic freedom that his or her colleagues enjoy at a small liberal arts college. We acknowledge this point, but are not convinced that every individual must march to the same configuration. Indeed, if we look hard enough, we can see "configuration proliferation" within TCUs. Although most individuals support some unions, for example, few individuals make the claim that every individual in America who works should be a member of a union. Rather, a common challenge appears to be how to structure policy to ensure that both FPCUs and TCUs enable faculty to perform to the best of their ability.

References

Adelman, C. (2000). A parallel universe: Certification in the information technology guild. *Change, 32*(3), 20–29.

Benjamin, E. (Ed.). (2003). Exploring the role of contingent instructional staff in undergraduate learning. *New Directions for Higher Education, 123*. San Francisco: Jossey-Bass.

Berg, G. A. (2005). Lessons from the edge: For-profit and nontraditional higher education in America. New York: Praeger.

Blumenstyk, G. (2004, October 8). U. of Phoenix pressure in recruiting, report says. *The Chronicle of Higher Education,* p. A1.

Dewey, J. (1936). The social significance of academic freedom. *Social Frontier, 2,* 165–167.

Fager, J. (Executive Producer). (2005, January 30). *60 Minutes* [Television broadcast]. New York: Columbia Broadcasting System.

Floyd. C. E. (2005). For-profit degree granting colleges: Who are these guys and what do they mean for students, traditional institutions, and public policy? In J. C. Smart (Ed.), *Higher education: Handbook of theory and research,* vol. 20 (pp. 539–590). Dordrecht, The Netherlands: Springer.

Harsanyl, D. (2005, December 29). DeVry ticked at kvetching on prof blog. *Denver Post.* Retrieved February 2, 2006, from http://www.denverpost.com.

Lechuga, V. M. (2006). *The changing landscape of the academic profession: The culture of faculty at for-profit colleges and universities.* New York: Routledge.

Makdisi, S. (2006, January 22). Witch hunt at UCLA. *Los Angeles Times,* p. M1.

Merrill Lynch. (2005, January). *Education and training services: Negative 60 Minutes piece finally airs.* (Flashnote 31 January 2005). New York: Sara Gubbins.

Metzger, W. (1955). *Academic freedom in the age of the university.* New York: Columbia University Press.

National Center for Education Statistics. (2001). *Digest for education statistics, 2001.* Washington, DC: U.S. Department of Education.

Rudolph, F. (1962). *The American college and university: A history.* New York: Knopf.

Schrecker, E. (1983). Academic freedom: The historical view. In C. Kaplan & E. Schrecker (Eds.), *Regulating the intellectuals* (pp. 27–29). New York: Praeger.

Slaughter, S. (1980). The danger zone: Academic freedom and civil liberties. *The ANNALS of the American Academy of Political and Social Science, 448,* 4661.

Tierney, W. G. (Ed.). (2004). *Competing conceptions of academic governance: Negotiating the perfect storm.* Baltimore: Johns Hopkins University Press.

Tierney, W. G., & Lechuga, V. M. (2005). Academic freedom in the 21st century. *Thought and Action, 21,* 7–22.

U.S. Department of Education. (2003). *Program review report: University of Phoenix* (PRCN 200340922254). Washington, DC: Author.

5

MARKETS, REGULATION, AND PERFORMANCE IN HIGHER EDUCATION

Mark L. Pelesh

I n an era of deregulation, higher education is one of the last great heavily regulated industries. Indeed, notwithstanding its venerable traditions and shibboleths—e.g., the institutional autonomy, diversity of institutional missions, and freedom from federal intrusion that have made American higher education the "envy of the world"—it may be plausibly argued that twenty-first-century higher education, as we know it, could not exist but for the funding and regulatory regime provided by government (Ward, 2006; Will, 2007). The federal student aid programs created by the Higher Education Act of 1965 (HEA) provided more than $83 billion in 2008—approximately 60 percent of all student aid and 23 percent of all higher education expenditures (National Center for Education Statistics, 2006). The regulatory environment stemming from this funding fundamentally shapes higher education.

This chapter will provide a description of the extensive regulatory system for higher education and how it came to be, place the FPCUs within that system, and offer an assessment of the interplay between markets and regulation and the trends driving the evolution of both. We will review the "Triad" of regulators—the federal government, states, and accrediting agencies—and how it has evolved since the G.I. Bill and the enactment of the HEA and its subsequent reauthorizations. We will then consider the place of FPCUs in the regulatory system—their inclusion in the HEA programs, but their distinctive treatment in certain key respects that qualifies their status as full and equal participants in higher education. As FPCUs have grown and thrived, conflicts over their status have become more acute in the legislative and regulatory arena. This, in turn, illustrates a key point about the subject of this chapter: the pervasiveness of regulation in higher education means that institutions compete in important ways through their engagement with legislation and regulation.

The Triad of Regulation

The basic structure of regulation of institutions of higher education, including FPCUs, consists of a "Triad" of the federal government, operating through the U.S. Department of Education, the states, and private accrediting agencies (Higher Education Act [HEA], 2007). The Department of Education's role focuses principally on the proper administration of the funding programs authorized by the HEA. It determines the eligibility of institutions to participate in those programs and, through regulation under the HEA, sets the terms and conditions of participation (HEA, 2007). The states provide institutions with the legal authority to operate and often focus on consumer protection. Many states also administer their own financial aid programs and, through them, set terms and conditions affecting how institutions operate (Kaplin & Lee, 1995). Finally, the accrediting agencies perform, to a greater or lesser extent, a regulatory role that principally focuses on educational quality. While the accrediting agencies are private entities, usually organized as nonprofit associations, their peer review and voluntary qualities have been heavily impinged by their roles as federally recognized gatekeepers to the HEA funding programs (Havighurst, 1994).

This triad has evolved over the last fifty years. While some antecedents may be found as far back as the nineteenth century, the G.I. Bill of 1952 began to shape the system that is recognizable today. It provided significant new funding that gave veterans access to higher education in unprecedented numbers. This program also created a need to ensure that the funds were spent on institutions and educational programs of sufficient quality, yet without direct federal involvement in oversight of educational content. A solution was found in existing private accrediting agencies, which set quality standards that conferred academic legitimacy upon the institutions and programs they accredited. Reliance upon the accrediting agencies, however, required that the federal government list those it recognized as "reliable authority as to the quality of the training offered by an educational institution"—otherwise, the problem of "fly-by-night" schools would simply be transferred to "fly by night" accreditors (Finkin, 1994, pp. 89, 93–98). This set in motion a tension in the relationship between the federal government and the accrediting agencies—and, by extension, the institutions they accredit. Institutional autonomy, on the one hand, and governmental demands for accountability for the effective use of taxpayer funds, on the other, are competing, if not wholly inconsistent, concepts. This tension continues to this day and has drawn both the accrediting agencies and institutions into a tighter federal embrace.

The next key event in the evolution of the higher education regulatory system was the HEA of 1965. This and other subsequent legislation greatly expanded the funding for student financial assistance, and built upon the concept of institutional eligibility. Similarly, in order to avoid direct federal involvement in matters of educational content and quality, reliance on recognized accrediting agencies was continued (Finkin, 1994). The HEA of 1965 also established an objective for the federal student aid programs—the education and training of students for productive involvement in the economy. In justifying the increased and ongoing spending of this Great Society program, proponents focused on "how best to increase the supply of trained manpower" and on the need for "competent, well-trained professional and technical personnel." Moreover, training for "gainful employment in a recognized occupation" was among the objectives that eligible institutions could pursue (U.S. Code Congressional and Administrative News, 1965). This notion of training for national economic purposes had been at work in the G.I. Bill as well.

FPCUs in time became eligible for the Guaranteed Student Loan and Pell Grant programs established by the HEA, albeit through a separate category of "institution of higher education." This definition is crucial, since under the HEA, students who attend eligible institutions of higher education may receive federal student financial aid. The definition of an "institution of higher education" is thus critical. The HEA contains a general definition, which does not include FPCUs, and another definition for purposes of the Title IV student loan and grant programs, which does include FPCUs (HEA, 2007). Thus, FPCUs are not considered institutions of higher education for all purposes under the HEA.

Accordingly, by the early 1970s, the main elements of the regulatory framework for higher education as we know it today were in place. Funding was to go to students, not directly to institutions, and criteria were developed to establish the eligibility of institutions at which students could utilize this funding. To avoid a federal ministry of education similar to those in other countries with more centralized, top-down oversight of educational content, reliance upon recognized private accrediting agencies was employed, as was a requirement for state authority to offer postsecondary education. With three regulators at work—the U.S. Department of Education and its predecessors, the states, and private accrediting agencies—the higher education regulatory system had role differentiation, but also a strong likelihood of overlap and possible conflict. The magnitude of the funding available—$83 billion in 2008, about 63 percent of all student aid—plus the economic objectives articulated at the outset of the programs made it likely that there would be periodic calls for accountability and transparency so that the taxpayers could be assured that their money was being well spent.

The process for "reauthorization" of the HEA programs ensured that this would be so: roughly every five years, Congress has revisited and revised the HEA to take into account new developments, problems, and trends, utilizing the concepts of institutional eligibility and participation in the aid programs as the hook for changing or adding requirements. The department, the states, and accrediting agencies, in turn, have changed their regulations, requirements, and standards in response.

In 1992, a watershed reauthorization took place driven by widely reported instances of misuse of federal student aid funds and soaring default rates on federally guaranteed student loans. These problems were concentrated, but were not exclusively, in the FPCU sector. (See, for example, Higher Education Amendments of 1992; U.S. Department of Education, 1994). Criticisms were leveled at each of the regulators in the student aid system for lax oversight and administration. For example, the Nunn Committee, the Senate Permanent Subcommittee on Investigations, in a report issued in 1991, called the Department of Education's record "dismal" in, among other things, lax and delayed re-certification of institutions to participate in the financial aid programs. The Nunn Committee also found the states had failed in their roles through lack of uniform standards, fragmented responsibility, inadequate staff and resources, and allowing political considerations to affect their oversight. And accreditation, especially for FPCUs, came in for severe criticism for inadequate standards and procedures, conflicts of interest, and a disinclination to serve as the gatekeeper for the Title IV programs that Congress and regulators expected (S. Rep. No. 102-58, 1991).

As a result, Congress mandated extensive changes to the HEA aimed at strengthening the triad regulatory system and eliminating the eligibility and participation of institutions that failed to meet tests for institutional integrity and quality. These new measures included, among others, caps on student loan default rates, institutional financial responsibility tests, limitations on the payment of incentive compensation to those involved in student recruiting and the award of financial aid, satisfactory academic progress requirements, and quasi–pro rata refund requirements. They also included completion and placement requirements for short-term programs, standards for minimum program length, limitations on branching of institutions, and new monitoring and swifter enforcement tools for the Department of Education (Higher Education Amendments of 1992).

These new federal measures were broadly applicable to all institutions of higher education, with eligibility to participate in the student aid programs acting as the lever to force changes in institutional behavior. While the Nunn Committee and other Congressional hearings found problems in all sectors of higher education, a recurrent theme was purported fraud and abuse at FPCUs. Thus, FPCUs had measures directed specifically at them through changes in the definition of a "proprietary institution of higher education"— the key to establishing their eligibility. Two of these were the elaboration of a "two-year rule," which required that FPCUs must function for two years before they could become eligible to participate in the federal student aid programs, and the creation of a rule requiring that FPCUs derive a minimum of 15 percent of their revenues from outside the aid programs (HEA, 59 Fed. Reg. 22,324, 22,327-29, 1994).

Congress addressed the other two legs of the triad as well. The most significant and lasting changes were those directed at accrediting agencies. As a condition to recognition by the federal government, accrediting agencies were required to be "separate and independent" of related institutional and professional associations, because the latter were believed to exert undue and inappropriate influence over accreditation standards and processes. In sum, Congress determined that the regulated agencies, through their trade associations, had obtained control of their federal funding gatekeeper regulators, the accrediting agencies. In addition to a structural divorce from these organizations, accrediting agencies were required to adopt standards and procedures to address new statutory mandates. Many of these concerned areas that overlapped with responsibilities given to the Department of Education—program length, completion and placement, and branching, for example. Others had an explicit tie to the administration of the student aid programs—default rates and compliance with the newly enacted federal aid program responsibilities, for example—and required the accrediting agencies to disclose actions they took and information they learned that had pertinence to the responsibilities of what were now referred to as their triad partners (Pelesh, 1994).

Just as with the new federal requirements applicable to institutions, the new federal requirements for accrediting agencies could not be directly imposed. Rather, the connection to the federal aid programs was again employed: accrediting agencies could not be recognized (i.e., approved) as gatekeepers for their accredited institutions to access the aid programs unless the accreditors met these new requirements. In addition, Congress sought to strengthen the recognition process conducted by the Department of Education (Pelesh, 1994). As previously noted, the department and its predecessors had long maintained a list of accrediting agencies considered reliable authorities on educational quality for purposes of federal student aid programs. This necessitated creating and administering a process for determining the accrediting agencies worthy of inclusion on the list. Based on the findings of the Nunn Committee, Congress now became much more prescriptive as to how the department would recognize accrediting agencies for inclusion, mandating a form of administrative hearing process that contemplated denials and revocation of recognition.

State regulatory responsibilities were also addressed in the amendments to the HEA enacted in the 1992 reauthorization. Owing to the structure of the federal system, however, the statutory possibilities were more limited. The 1992 amendments created a new State Postsecondary Review Program to be funded by the federal government, with something called a State Postsecondary Review Entity (SPRE) in each state to administer it. The SPREs' responsibilities overlapped to a considerable degree with those of the Department of Education and accrediting agencies in such areas as utilization of default rates as review triggers and assessment of student outcomes (Pelesh, 1994). As it turned out, the SPRE initiative was short-lived; Congress eliminated it after the Republican takeover of Congress in 1994 (see the HEA P.L. No. 105-244). As we will see, this episode prefigured how FPCUs and TCUs approach regulation in higher education. While FPCUs were gravely concerned about the SPREs and initially sought to neutralize them, the FPCUs quickly pivoted and moved to work with the SPREs once it appeared that they would begin to function. The TCUs, in contrast, consistently opposed the SPREs and convinced the new Republican majority leadership that they were an example of excessive and dangerous government regulation.

The other changes that Congress made in 1992 have proven to be more lasting. When the HEA was next reauthorized in 1998, the amendments involved fine-tuning rather than major change. Thus, for example, the requirement that FPCUs obtain a minimum percentage of their revenues outside the student aid programs was modified from 15 percent to 10 percent (H. Conference Rep. No. 105-750 at 9, 1998). But the much-enhanced regulatory system established in 1992 was left largely intact (H. Conference Rep., 1998). Congress has just completed another reauthorization in the summer of 2008. Again, it maintained the contours of the regulatory structure, with certain modifications. In fact, in responses to rising bipartisan concerns about the rising cost of higher education and calls for transparency and accountability, Congress enhanced the system by creating extensive new reporting requirements for institutions of higher education.

FPCUs in the Regulatory System

The place of FPCUs in this regulatory system, as indicated above, has distinctive, if not entirely distinct, features. To begin with, FPCUs have their own definition as an institution of higher education. That definition is the key to unlocking the federal treasury, and the separate definition for FPCUs places them on a different footing from other public and private nonprofit institutions. The FPCU definition has special conditions and requirements not applicable to traditional colleges and universities—most especially the 90/10 rule, which limits FPCUs, and them alone, on the percentage of revenues they may obtain from the Title IV programs.

It has been a goal of the Career College Association (CCA), the national association representing many of the FPCUs, in reauthorizations since 1992 to have a single definition of an institution of higher education in the HEA (Career College Association, 2005). The CCA contends that such a step would recognize the evolution of higher education and the maturation of FPCUs, eliminate a source of confusion that multiple definitions cause, and refocus the HEA on its original core purpose—support for students, not institutions, as they prepare for productive involvement in the economy. Opponents of a single definition focus on what they perceive as inherent differences between types of institutions and contend that dual definitions will appropriately direct federal resources to institutions they believe "will best serve society" (Heller, 2003; Moore, 2003). In the reauthorization of the HEA completed in the summer of 2008, the single definition goal was unrealized.

The battle over the single definition was indicative of a larger clash relating to the status of FPCUs in higher education. The FPCUs have long sought recognition as legitimate and equivalent participants to the TCUs. That desire has gained importance as, by FPCUs' lights, they have moved beyond the deficiencies that fueled the reforms of the 1992 reauthorization. TCU representatives, however, have resisted the FPCUs' achievement of this goal. While there were other objections lodged against specifics of the single definition proposal, at bottom, the TCU opposition was fundamentally a resistance to according the FPCUs the equivalent status they seek. As matters stand after the 2008 reauthorization, FPCUs still are not "institutions of higher education" as generally defined by the HEA. They continue to have their own definition that is applicable only to the Title IV programs and that focuses on their for-profit status.

Other HEA requirements, while applicable to all institutions, have tended to fall more heavily on FPCUs. The cohort default rate regime is a clear example. While all institutions may be rendered ineligible if the default rates of their former students exceed caps of 25 percent over three consecutive years, the majority of institutions that lost eligibility in the 1990s after the caps were instituted were FPCUs. And, in the 2008 reauthorization, cohort default rates flared as an issue again in ways that showed their disproportionate impact on FPCUs. TCU representatives advanced a proposal to change how default rates would be calculated, the effect of which would have been to dramatically and immediately increase the default rates of all institutions, but most likely push the rates of FPCUs over the 25 percent cap. FPCUs led the opposition to this proposal and ultimately achieved a compromise that included a transitional period to the new method of calculation and an increase in the cap to 30 percent.

The incentive compensation prohibition for those involved in student recruitment is arguably similar to cohort default rates as a requirement falling more heavily on FPCUs. FPCUs have tended to be more explicit, if not more aggressive, than their more traditional counterparts about their sales and marketing efforts, many of which are impelled by a need to fill classroom seats, too.

Regulatory treatment of FPCUs by the states and accrediting agencies can also be distinctive. In some states, such as Texas, regulation of institutions of higher education has been done on a two-tier basis, with one regulatory body governing nondegree, workforce-oriented institutions and another body overseeing degree-granting, traditional academic institutions (Tex. Ed. Code, 2002). Other states, such as California and Florida, have explicitly provided for exemptions from regulation or special privileges to access state financial aid programs for regionally accredited institutions (Ca. Ed. Code §§ 69430, 94739(b)(7); Florida Statutes, 2008).

For-profit ownership structure has not been an explicit qualification for whether an institution is eligible for accreditation for some time, and could not be under the antitrust laws. Such a criterion would amount to a group boycott or concerted refusal to deal among competitors and violate section 1 of the Sherman Act (Jacobs, 1992, pp. 11–12; *United States* v. *American Bar Assn.*, 1996). But the accredited populations of the recognized regional and national accrediting agencies have tended to divide roughly along the lines of ownership structure, with the vast majority of public and private nonprofit institutions accredited by one of the six regionals and almost all of the nationally accredited institutions being FPCUs (Imagine America Foundation, 2007; Von Alt, 2007). The division is not complete, however; some FPCUs, including those owned by some of the largest publicly traded companies, have regional accreditation, such as the University of Phoenix, DeVry, and Strayer (Imagine America Foundation, 2007; Von Alt, 2007).

While both regional and national accrediting agencies are recognized under the HEA and in theory meet the same regulatory requirements for recognition, regional and national approaches and standards have differed in some important ways. Moreover, the department's recognition process has not always held the regional and national accreditors to the same requirements. This is most clearly seen in the area of student achievement standards. National accrediting agencies have been compelled to adopt quantitative standards, usually some form of minimum rates, for completion and placement (59 Fed. Reg.). The regional accrediting agencies, in contrast, have not had to adopt such standards and instead utilize a much different process-oriented approach that assesses whether their accredited institutions are themselves appropriately setting goals for student achievement and measuring against those goals.

In the recognition process, the department has to date permitted the regional accrediting agencies to utilize this more subjective, nonquantitative approach to student achievement, even though there is no statutory basis for such disparate treatment (Lederman, 2007a; 2007b). On the contrary, Congress emphasized the importance of student achievement in the recognition of accrediting agencies in the 1998 reauthorization (64 Fed. Reg. 34,466, 34,469, 1999). Moreover, the disparate treatment cannot be justified on the basis of the institutions accredited by the different accreditors; the regional agencies accredit FPCUs and other institutions offering programs whose mission is to prepare individuals for entry or advancement in the workforce as much as the institutions accredited by the national agencies. And the profit motive of agencies' accredited institutions is simply not part of the accrediting agency recognition criteria.

The untenability of the differential treatment in this score led finally to an initiative in 2007 from the Department of Education, arising from the work of Secretary Margaret Spellings' Commission on the Future of Higher Education, to call for objective quantitative assessment of student achievement by all accrediting agencies. The national accrediting agencies and FPCUs supported this initiative; the regional accrediting agencies and TCUs opposed it. At their behest, Congressional leaders halted the department's initiative and then amended the HEA in the 2008 reauthorization to provide latitude for the regional accrediting agencies' approach.

With considerable justification, therefore, the FPCUs may chafe at aspects of the regulatory system that do treat them differently. From HEA requirements such as the 90/10 rule that imperil their continued existence to state rules that exclude them from more deferential regulatory treatment and funding programs to accreditation requirements that hold them to more exacting quantitative student achievement standards, FPCUs are, to some extent, treated as less than full-fledged participants in higher education. As previously indicated, this explains the drive by FPCUs for a single definition of an institution of higher education. If it could be achieved, such a definition would redress their sense of regulatory second-class citizenship.

Yet, FPCUs have proven their ability since the 1992 reauthorization to make a virtue of their regulatory circumstances. True, many FPCUs were removed from eligibility for the HEA student aid programs as a result of high cohort default rates, loss of accreditation, or other violations of the HEA and Department of Education regulations. But the FPCU segment of the higher education industry is robust and growing. FPCUs account for almost 40 percent of all postsecondary institutions eligible for the HEA student aid programs (National Center for Education Statistics, 2005). Between 1997 and 2005, the consolidated annual growth rate (CAGR) for student enrollments at all degree-granting institutions has been 2.4 percent. But for two-year FPCUs, the CAGR has been 5.2 percent, and for four-year FPCUs, it has been 21.7 percent. In contrast, the CAGR for private nonprofit and public four-year institutions has been only 2 percent, and for two-year public institutions, it has been even less—1.8 percent. Two-year private nonprofit institutions' student enrollments have actually declined 6.1 percent (National Center for Education Statistics, 2005). The picture for nondegree student enrollments is even more dramatic. The CAGR for FPCUs is 6 percent or greater, while private nonprofit and public institutions have generally seen declines ranging from 5.9 percent to 12.7 percent (National Center for Education Statistics, 2005). Revenues at FPCUs have also grown at a fast rate—14 percent over the last seven years (National Center for Education Statistics, 2005).

Thus, even though FPCUs still have a small share of the overall market for postsecondary education (approximately 10 percent) that share has been growing (from about 5 percent ten years ago) while other segments of the postsecondary education industry have been struggling to maintain share or declining. As a recent investment analysis put it: "As with the healthcare industry 30 years ago, private providers at all levels are gaining share at the expense of publicly-funded institutions through greater ingenuity, innovation, and efficiency" (Urdan & Lee, 2007). It goes on to say that the growth in enrollments among FPCUs "has not simply been through market expansion but has been driven by capacity constraints in public four-year institutions as well as declines in the comparative appeal of not-for-profit, private two-year institutions . . . . There also appears to be clear recognition by the market that for-profit programs are superior to those offered by public and not-for-profit schools" (Urdan & Lee, 2007, p. 4).

Clearly, FPCUs have learned not only to survive, but also to thrive, in what appeared would be a generally tougher regulatory environment after the 1992 reauthorization, with important aspects of that environment particularly tilted against FPCUs. Indeed, there is a sense in which the features of the regulatory system have worked to the advantage of FPCUs—not because they have been too lax, but precisely because they have been so difficult. New entrants face high hurdles in the form of securing accreditation, which is a multiyear process, and the two-year rule. Competition to existing players is thus limited. Once in the system, the extensiveness of the regulatory require-ments and the pervasiveness of the regulators' scrutiny require a substantial investment in regulatory compliance in order to avoid multiple potent threats to the FPCUs' business. The Department of Education, a state, or an accred-iting agency are capable at any time of taking action that would close down a campus. This significant ongoing investment and attention to compliance thus likewise constitute barriers to new entrants, and ways by which existing competitors may be eliminated apart from head-to-head competition.

In addition, to the extent that regulation does bear a relationship to insti-tutional quality and integrity, it may have improved FPCU performance and helped make them successful. The differences in how FPCUs are measured against student achievement standards is the clearest example. As noted above, after the 1992 reauthorization, only the national accrediting agencies, which accredit the bulk of the FPCUs, were obliged to adopt objective quan-titative standards to measure completion and placement rates. Perhaps prov-ing the position articulated by a former Inspector General of the Department of Education that one only gets what one measures, the average completion rate for associate degree students at FPCUs was 60.1 percent, while the aver-age completion rate for such students at public institutions (usually commu-nity colleges) was 24.1 percent. (National Center for Education Statistics, 2004, p. 11). The disparity for bachelor's degree students was not as great, but—tellingly—the trend lines began to diverge in 1995, just after the Department of Education promulgated its student achievement regulations for accrediting agencies (Urdan & Lee, 2007). No comprehensive national data on placement rates exist that would permit a comparison between FPCUs and other institutions, even though surveys consistently place future employment as a crucial concern and objective of incoming freshmen at all institutions (Higher Education Research Institute, 2006, pp. 2–3).

Thus, differential regulation may have worked to the FPCUs' advantage. As tuition increases in traditional higher education institutions continue to outpace inflation and calls for accountability for results from the public's investment are heard, especially in regard to completion rates, FPCUs can claim that they are already measured for the results that matter most to prospective students and their families—whether students complete and get a job in the fields for which they have been educated and trained under objective, quantitative standards. This very accountability takes policymakers back to the foundations for the student aid programs as articulated by the proponents of the HEA when it was enacted. What was initially seen as a double standard, in another view, provides a focus and discipline that affords the FPCUs marketplace and public policy advantages.

Regulation and Competition

This suggests that unlike other industries, the paradigm of debate for higher education and FPCUs is not regulation versus deregulation, but rather what kind of regulation should be imposed, and to what ends. With the HEA student aid programs representing almost one-quarter of annual postsecondary revenues (not to mention additional substantial funding coming from public research grants and state appropriations to public institutions) it would be unrealistic to expect that government would, or could ever, choose to deregulate and allow competition among institutions principally to set the terms and conditions of how this taxpayer financing should accrue to the benefit of suppliers and consumers. And, in fact, none of the participants in the regulatory system would seriously consider arguing for such an approach. True, there is a certain degree of reflexive rhetoric against government intrusion on the part of TCUs, on the one hand, and criticism of government bureaucracy on the part of the more business-oriented FPCUs, on the other. But these are more comfortable tropes reflective of the viewpoints of their institutional leaders than they are serious advocacy for fundamental legislative change.

Rather, working largely within the confines of the regulatory system that has evolved, higher education institutions seek to use legislative and regulatory processes at least as much, if not more than, the marketplace to compete with one another. Only this can explain why advocates for TCU interests would make the retention and strengthening of the 90/10 rule one of the elements of their legislative program in the current reauthorization (Ward, 2006). On its face, this rule has no impact on public and private nonprofit institutions, as the requirement to secure a minimum percentage of revenues from outside the HEA student aid programs does not apply to them and only applies to FPCUs. As a measure to threaten or eliminate FPCUs, however— which have been making increasing claims on the pool of available federal student aid funding—it makes good sense.

Competition through the regulatory system is also why TCU representatives would so strenuously resist proposals like those for a single definition of an institution of higher education. Their opposition was even more strident to an FPCU proposal for a prohibition in the HEA against institutions refusing even to consider credits for transfer from nationally accredited institutions (American Association of Collegiate Registrars and Administrative Officers). Neither would likely have a material impact on traditional institutions' finances or operations. But they would send signals that FPCUs have arrived as equally legitimate options for students, while retention of a separate definition and preservation of institutions' ability to discriminate based on accreditation that most FPCUs do not have would continue to give traditional institutions a status sanctioned by the statute and regulations, with marketplace advantages.

The FPCUs also utilize the legislative and regulatory processes for competitive advantage. Their positions on the single definition issue and transfer of credit are exactly the converse of those described above for TCUs and would, if achieved, confer the marketplace advantages that TCUs fear. In addition, FPCUs' willingness to support calls for accountability for student achievement plays to their strength and against the inability of traditional institutions thus far to provide meaningful data on what the investment of significant public and familial resources yields in terms of measurable student achievement. In recent years, demographic and economic trends have provided a powerful impetus to the advocacy agenda of FPCUs. These have included increasing student mobility, the predominance of the "nontraditional" student, and fears about worsening national economic competitiveness, partly driven by concern about poor student performance and preparation for the workforce at all levels (Secretary of Education's Commission on the Future of Higher Education, 2006, pp. vii–x).

The vicissitudes of political competition between the major parties can also play an important role. FPCUs found a relatively receptive ear during the period of Republican control of the Congress. Since those associated with TCUs are among the most reliable constituencies of the Democratic party, the receptiveness of the Congress to the FPCUs' agenda and point of view after the 2006 elections which changed control of Congress was more in question. Once again, however, the adaptability of FPCUs was evident as they worked with the new Democratic majority leaders on the cohort default rate compromise previously described and on changes to the 90/10 rule that will allow FPCUs to include additional types of revenues to comply with the rule, beyond even those that Congress under Republican leadership had contemplated.

The fortunes of all institutions of higher education, including FPCUs, are therefore powerfully affected by the system for regulation. With their business funded substantially by the government, layers of regulation have developed to maintain some level of accountability for the use of this funding. Those regulatory demands have tended to grow over time as education becomes second only to healthcare as a component of gross domestic product (GDP) and paramount to future personal and national prosperity. Leaders of FPCUs and other institutions of higher education thus have little choice but to engage in the rough and tumble of the legislative and regulatory processes—and perhaps much to gain if they do so shrewdly.

References

Abuses in Federal Student Aid Programs, S. Rep. No. 102-58 (1991).

American Association of Collegiate Registrars and Administrative Officers (AACRAO), Federalizing Transfer of Academic Credit, www.aacrao.org.

Ca. Ed. Code §§ 69430, 94739(b)(7).

Career College Association (2005). 2005 *Higher education agenda*. www.career.org.

Finkin, M. (1994). The unfolding tendency in the federal relationship to private accreditation in higher education. *Law and Contemporary Problems, 57*(4), 89–120.

Florida Statutes, Title XLVIII, § 1009.89 (2008).

H. Conference Rep. No. 105-750 (1998).

Havighurst, C. C. (1994). Private accreditation in the regulatory state. *Law and Contemporary Problems, 57.*

Heller, D. (2003, November 14). Not all institutions are alike. *The Chronicle of Higher Education.* Retrieved September 30, 2008, from http://chronicle.com/weekly/v50/i12/12b00702.htm.

Higher Education Amendments of 1992, P.L. 102-325 (July 23, 1992); H. Rep. No. 102-447 (1992).

Higher Education Act, 59 Fed. Reg. 22,324, 22,327-29, 1994.

Higher Education Act, 20 U.S.C. §1099; 34 C.F.R. §§600, 668 (2007).

Higher Education Act P.L. No. 105-244.

Higher Education Research Institute (2006). *The American freshman: Forty year trends 1966–2006.* Retrieved September 30, 2008, from www.gseis.ucla.edu/heri/40yrtrends.php.

Imagine America Foundation (2007). *2007 Fact Book: A Profile of Career Colleges and Universities.* Retrieved September 30, 2008, from www.imagine-america.org/pdfs/2007IAFFactBook.pdf.

Institutional Eligibility Under the Higher Education Act of 1965, as Amended, 59 Fed. Reg. 22,324, 22,327-29 (April 29, 1994).

Jacobs, J. (1992). *Certification and accreditation law handbook.* Washington, DC: American Society of Association Executives.

Kaplin, W. A., & Lee, B.A. (1995). *The law of higher education.* San Francisco: Jossey-Bass.

Lederman, D. (2007a, December 19). Someone didn't get the memo. *Inside Higher Ed.* Retrieved January 20, 2008, from www.insidehighered.com/news/2007/12/19/naciqi.

Lederman, D. (2007b, December 20). Fundamental Differences, *Inside Higher Ed.* Retrieved January 20, 2008, from www.insidehighered.com/news/2007/12/20/naciqi.

Moore, D.G. (2003, November 14). Toward a single definition of college. *The Chronicle of Higher Education.* Retrieved September 30, 2008, from http://chronicle.com/weekly/v50/i12/12b00701.htm.

National Center for Education Statistics (2004). *Enrollment in Postsecondary Institutions.* Retrieved September 30, 2008, from http://nces.ed.gov/pubs2006/2006155.pdf.

National Center for Education Statistics (2005). Institutional characteristics. Retrieved September 30, 2008, from http://nces.ed.gov/IPEDS/.

National Center for Education Statistics (2006). *Digest of education statistics.* Retrieved September 30, 2008, from http://nces.ed.gov/Programs/digest/.

Pelesh, M. (1994). Regulations under the Higher Education Amendments of 1992: A case study in negotiated rulemaking. *Law and Contemporary Problems, 57*(4), 151–170.

Secretary of Education's Commission on the Future of Higher Education (2006). *A test of leadership: Charting the future of U.S. higher education.* Washington, DC: Author.

Secretary's Recognition of Accrediting Agencies, 64 Fed. Reg. 34,466, 34,469 (June 25, 1999).

Tex. Ed. Code Chapter 132, § 61.301 et seq. (2002).

Urdan, T., & Lee, J. (2007). *2007 post-secondary fact book.* Washington, DC: Signal Hill. http://hosting.bronto.com/1902/public/2007-11-28_Post_Secondary_Fact_Book.pdf

United States v. *American Bar Assn.,* 934 F.Supp. 435 (D.D.C. 1996).

U.S. Code Congressional and Administrative News 4053 (1965).

U.S. Department of Education. (1994). Secretary's Procedures and Criteria for Recognition of Accrediting Agencies, 59 Fed. Reg. 22,250, 22,264.

U.S. Department of Education. (2008). *Financial aid.* Retrieved September 30, 2008, from www.ed.gov/finaid.

Von Alt, K. A. (2007). *Accredited institutions of postsecondary education.* Washington, DC: American Council on Education.

Ward, D. (2006). Statement of American Council on Education president David Ward on the final meeting of the Spellings Commission on the Future of Higher Education. Retrieved September 30, 2008, from www.acenet.edu/AM/Template.cfm ?Section=Press_Releases2&CONTENTID=17767&TEMPLATE=/CM/Content Display.cfm.

Will, K. H. (2007, October 4). Opposing view: "The envy of the world." *USA Today.* Retrieved September 30, 2008, from http://blogs.usatoday.com/oped/2007/10/ opposing-view-t.html.

6

ACCREDITATION AND ACCOUNTABILITY

The Role of For-Profit Education and National Accrediting Agencies

Elise Scanlon and Michale S. McComis

The accountability movement in education has reached a fever pitch. From the passage of the No Child Left Behind Act in 2002 to the reauthorization of the Higher Education Act in 2008, the debate in the education community and the federal government has centered around holding educational institutions accountable for the education they deliver. In the for-profit education sector, this debate happened a decade earlier with a previous reauthorization of the Higher Education Act (HEA) and moved the for-profit education community and accrediting agencies such as the Accrediting Commission of Careers Schools and Colleges of Technology toward a student-centered, student achievement, and outcomes-based model of educational delivery, oversight, and accountability.

When the issue of accountability in higher education reared its head under the George W. Bush administration, the for-profit postsecondary school sector was not the focus, as it had been in the early 1990s; rather, the traditional higher education community (i.e., not-for-profit 4-year community colleges, colleges, and universities) came under scrutiny for not holding itself accountable for the delivery of education. Although previously decried by the federal government in the early 1990s for unscrupulous practices, the for-profit sector would serve as a resource and example for the federal government to show how accrediting agencies and their accredited institutions can work together to foster accountability in education.

This chapter first lays out the history of one national accrediting agency, the Accrediting Commission of Careers Schools and Colleges of Technology (ACCSCT),[1] and its path toward achieving a student-centered and accountability-based model of accreditation. Secondly, the chapter describes the new accountability debate as it occurred under the G. W. Bush administration, and the new role that national accreditation served in that debate.

The Higher Education Act of 1965

The Dawn of a New Era in For-Profit Education and Accreditation

President Lyndon Johnson's domestic agenda, his "Great Society," included landmark educational funding legislation—the Higher Education Act of 1965. The Higher Education Act was the first explicit federal commitment to increase access to college for low-income students and created the Educational Opportunity Grants and the Guaranteed Student Loan (GSL) program and opened access for federal funding to both public and private (e.g., for-profit) postsecondary institutions. In addition, the Higher Education Act strengthened the link between access to federal funds and accreditation. Although an attenuated link between federal funding for higher education and accreditation had first been established with the passage of the Serviceman's Opportunity Act in 1944, the Higher Education Act's reliance on accreditation as a gatekeeper to the access of federal funds highly incentivized postsecondary institutions to seek and obtain accreditation (Millard, 1983).

The for-profit postsecondary school sector, having been previously excluded from access to federal funding initiatives for higher education, began to mobilize in 1965 as a means to achieve participation in federal funding initiatives and to seek greater legitimacy of the industry. In March 1965, owners of for-profit postsecondary institutions came together to discuss the formation of a national association and accreditation agency for their industry. The theme of that meeting was the need to create an accrediting agency that represented "high standards" and "quality education [as a] cornerstone" as a means to instill confidence in the for-profit postsecondary institution sector of education and to garner access to the new federal funding opportunity of the Higher Education Act (Baxandall & Cooney, 1983, p. 549).

After this initial meeting in 1965, a group of postsecondary for-profit institutions formed the National Association of Trade and Technical Schools (NATTS). Although NATTS served as both the trade association for the industry as well as the source of accreditation, early on, accreditation was a primary focus of the organization. Within a year of the formation of NATTS, the organization had created a process to obtain accreditation and a set of accreditation standards and input requirements as a means to evaluate educational quality and institutional accountability. At the 2nd Annual Convention of NATTS in 1966, William Goddard, the Executive Director of NATTS, indicated that accreditation was the association's "immediate thrust" to achieve a "respected place in the emerging educational system of America [and to] "achieve the excellence necessary to stay there" (Kempfer & Kempfer, 1966, p. 8).

On August 24, 1967, NATTS received provisional designation as a federally recognized national accrediting agency that could thereby act as a gatekeeper to the funds authorized by the Higher Education Act. By 1969, the federal Accreditation Institutional Eligibility staff lauded NATTS' demonstrated ability to help school operations improve their institutions (Accreditation Institutional Eligibility, 1969). NATTS was created with an intention to set high standards and to hold its accredited institutions accountable for meeting those standards. The early model of NATTS accreditation, as with many accreditation systems, however, was based largely on institutional input requirements, and while accountability was a part of this system, accountability in terms of quantitative student achievement outcomes would not become a central part of the organization's accreditation paradigm for three decades.

Generally, accountability in education began to receive far greater attention with the 1983 publication of *A Nation at Risk* by the National Commission on Excellence in Education. In the early 1980s President Reagan had called for a significant reduction in federal education spending and for the dissolution of the U.S. Department of Education and a far less prominent role of the federal government in state-run education (Bell, 1986). *A Nation at Risk*, however, indicated that several deficiencies existed in all aspects of American education and persuasively abated any attempt that the Reagan administration could have made toward the dissolution of the U.S. Department of Education or the federal funding programs for education.

While *A Nation at Risk* did not directly address postsecondary vocational education, it did indicate that high schools were not preparing young people for the workplace at a time "when the demand for highly skilled workers in new fields is accelerating rapidly" and when "technology is radically transforming a host of occupations" (National Commission on Excellence in Education [NCEE], 1983, p. 10). The report stated that retraining was a necessary tool needed for the nation to thrive and prosper, and that high school curricula needed to include occupational endeavors in order to advance student career goals. *A Nation at Risk* called for a commitment by the nation to enhance quality in education and student retention in schools and to better prepare students for life after schooling (NCEE, 1983). Many would argue that this report began the accountability movement in education and ultimately led to the No Child Left Behind Act of 2001.

For NATTS, the notion of accountability had already been established. The NATTS *Standards of Accreditation* reinforced the central principles of the organization and required its accredited institutions to demonstrate reasonable rates of program completion and job placement (Tolbert, 1979; NATTS, 1990). The level of student achievement accountability at this time, however, was highly subjective assessments; there were no established student achievement criteria or definition of "reasonable."

NATTS' accreditation mechanisms were also taxed in the 1980s as the information age dawned, and with it significantly greater reliance upon electronic technology. As industries grappled with the concepts of retraining and the need for workers with increased skills, for-profit postsecondary schools flourished. The sector was seen as providing viable opportunities for individuals in need of skills either as a means to enter the workforce or to keep pace with the changes brought on by the information age. Accordingly, NATTS experienced extreme growth starting in about 1980 and lasted throughout the 1980s. From 1980 to 1985, the number of NATTS-accredited institutions increased from 550 to 811, and the membership reached its peak of 1,257 by 1990 (see chapter Appendix A) (National Association of Trade and Technical Schools (NATTS), Accrediting Commission of Trade and Technical Schools (ACTTS), Accrediting Commission of Career Schools and Colleges of Technology (ACCSCT), 1966–2008). NATTS' accreditation processes and infrastructure, however, could not keep pace with the growth of its membership and the accountability of its accredited institutions suffered. Some of the extreme growth of the sector of schools in the 1980s led ultimately to widespread failures of corporate institutions, and some led to significant fraud and abuse of the federal funding programs established by the Higher Education Act of 1965 and the Job Training Partnership Act of 1982.

The original founders of NATTS had sought to bring legitimacy to its member institutions and to focus on quality in the industry. However, the organization simply could not keep pace with the ample opportunity for growth in the 1980s, and the accountability of its institutions waned. As one of the founders of NATTS stated:

> Some of the large corporations were much too energetic in their desire to fill up the seats and they started to hire outside salesmen in all states and they got carried away. Ethics became secondary considerations. High pressure sales and recruitment were the number one concern. They were bringing in students, promising the "blue sky" stuff, and that was the cause of a lot of problems. (Baxandall & Cooney, 1983, p. 485)

Although NATTS' mission had not changed, the focus of the organization and its ability to apply its quality assurance standards effectively did change dramatically. As the 1980s came to a close, the for-profit sector of postsecondary education, to include accreditation and NATTS in particular, would be called to task for the rapid proliferation of institutions in the sector and for what was perceived to be ineffective accountability measures in place to ensure the quality of education offered.

The 1992 Amendments to the Higher Education Act of 1965

The years leading up to the 1992 amendments to the Higher Education Act saw rapid—and, in many instances, unfettered—growth in the trade school sector. Accompanying this growth was fraud and abuse of federal financial assistance dollars by less than scrupulous for-profit school owners. Although fraud and abuse of federal funding was not representative of the entire sector of for-profit postsecondary education, the entire sector nevertheless was painted with the same broad brush and was labeled nothing but unscrupulous trade schools. From this depiction came a climate of mistrust of NATTS and its accreditation process, as well as allegations that the organization had not been holding its institutions accountable to standards and ethical business practices.

Prompted by reports of high student loan default rates and increasing instances of waste, fraud, and abuse in the federal student financial aid programs, the Chairman of the Senate Permanent Subcommittee on Investigation, Sam Nunn (D-GA), initiated an investigation of these reports in 1989, much of which focused on the for-profit sector. The subcommittee found

> overwhelming evidence that the [Guaranteed Student Loan program], particularly as it relates to proprietary schools, is riddled with fraud, waste, and abuse, and is plagued by substantial mismanagement and incompetence. Despite the acknowledged contributions of the well-intended, competent, and honest individuals and institutions comprising the large majority of GSLP participants, unscrupulous, inept, and dishonest elements among them have flourished throughout the 1980s. The latter have done so by exploiting both the ready availability of billions of dollars of Guaranteed Student Loans and the weak and inattentive system responsible for them [e.g., accreditation] leaving hundreds of thousands of students with little or no training, no jobs, and significant debt that they cannot possible repay. While those responsible have reaped huge profits, the American taxpayer has been left to pick up the tab for billions of dollars in attendant losses. (U.S. Senate, 1991, p. 6)

The subcommittee reported that inattention by accreditation led to rampant branching of institutions, inappropriate course length (i.e., stretching the duration of a course or program in order to secure greater amount of federal aid dollars), unethical practices in student recruitment and admission, and abuses in refunding appropriate tuition amounts both to students and the federal government. Moreover, the subcommittee reported that accreditation had "failed to assure that proprietary schools provide the quality of education required for GSL participation" (U.S. Senate, 1991, p. 15), that accreditation, particularly in the for-profit sector, was a mismatched regulatory concept, that accrediting agencies had not taken seriously their role as gatekeepers to federal dollars, that accreditation policies and procedures were inadequate to truly assess and promote quality, and that the accreditation system of self-regulation and peer review led to conflicts of interest and abuses of position. These findings would be chief among the elements that would be debated during the reauthorization of the Higher Education Act, and the 1992 amendments to this legislation would change the face and meaning of accountability for NATTS and the accreditation sector.

In 1992 Congress passed the reauthorization of the Higher Education Act. Congress greatly strengthened the U.S. Department of Education's ability to remove problem institutions from its aid programs but rejected proposals to bar for-profit institutions from participating in federal student financial assistance programs altogether because of the important role played by vocational postsecondary education in America. This decision notwithstanding, the impact of the 1992 amendments would mean that fewer schools, particularly those offering vocational education programs, would be eligible to participate in federal college aid programs.

The delivery of quality educational services and accountability measures addressed in the 1992 reauthorization of Higher Education Act included:

1. Efforts to curb loan defaults and other abuses in aid programs, making the schools responsible if students defaulted on their loans
2. Mandates to exclude schools with 50+ percent in correspondence courses from eligibility for aid programs; all correspondence schools must be aimed at traditional postsecondary degrees in order to be eligible for aid
3. Exclusion of schools from eligibility if they had filed for bankruptcy, or if owners had committed a crime involving aid programs
4. Beginnings of reviews of institutional eligibility for federal aid, particularly with respect to administrative and financial capacity
5. Requirements for accreditors of vocational educational institutions to create student achievement standards in the areas of completion, placement, and state licensure examination pass rates

The accountability measures for vocational education institutions under the new law took three distinct forms: first, accountability with respect to student loan default rates; second, accountability by institutions with respect to ensuring appropriate program length; third, accountability for accreditors and the requirement for agencies to have standards related to "bright-line" measurements for student program completion, job attainment, and state licensure examination pass rates. With these new accountability requirements in place, questions loomed as to whether accrediting agencies were capable or willing to hold institutions accountable in these areas, and to serve as a reliable indicator of an institution's educational quality as envisioned by the federal government.

There is no doubt that the 1992 amendments rendered many for-profit institutions ineligible to participate in the federal student financial aid programs, and that without that funding source for its students, those institutions could no longer operate as viable schools. As an example of this impact, the number of institutions accredited by NATTS dropped from 1,257 in 1990 to 968 in 1993—a 23 percent decrease in just three years. By 1997, the 30th anniversary of NATTS, this number had dropped to 864 (see chapter Appendix A) (NATTS, ACTTS, ACCSCT 1966–2008).

By 1993, NATTS as an organization had given way to its successor organization, the Accrediting Commission of Career Schools and Colleges of Technology. ACCSCT was completely independent of the trade association activities that had been a part of the NATTS organization. This separation allowed for ACCSCT to chart a new direction and to build new confidence in accreditation for the for-profit sector of education, dispelling any notion that the agency was not a reliable indicator of quality education

ACCSCT and Accountability Since 1990

Prior to the inception of ACCSCT, NATTS had standards requiring reasonable rates of student program completion and job attainment (NATTS, 1990). However, with the legislative changes brought about by the 1992 reauthorization of the Higher Education Act, which required accreditors for vocational education institutions to create student achievement standards in the areas of completion, placement, and state licensure examination pass rates, ACCSCT's standards would become more specific and quantitative and would represent a turning point in the organization's history of accountability and model of accreditation.

In 1990, NATTS had engaged in its first longitudinal assessment study of student outcomes, using the years 1987–1989. By 1994, ACCSCT had established a definition of program completion and a method of reporting rates of student program completion and employment after graduation in order to ensure uniformity among its accredited institutions. But ACCSCT did not alter its standards; it continued to measure student achievement in the post–1992 amendment era based upon its standards that institutions demonstrate "reasonable rates" of program completion and job placement. From 1993 through 1998, ACCSCT used "unspoken" and unpublished tripwires for reported program completion and job placement rates. Essentially, a 60 percent program completion rate or job placement rate would put a school into a student achievement "outcomes reporting" status with ACCSCT. But these rates were not actually required by the *Standards of Accreditation*, and this subjective process led to criticisms of ACCSCT's efforts in this area.

In 1994, the U.S. Department of Education Office of the Inspector General of the (OIG) conducted an audit of five select accrediting agencies, of which ACCSCT was one. Ultimately, the OIG found that

> The agencies were generally not using performance measures to effectively assess and improve the quality of education offered by member schools. While the agencies encouraged schools to evaluate the effectiveness of their programs, none of the agencies required a member school to stop offering an ineffective program. Only one of the agencies had quantified a minimum performance standard [not ACCSCT]. Additionally, all agencies did not adequately verify performance data reported by member schools. (U.S. Department of Education-Office of Inspector General, 1995, p. 1)

Thomas Bloom, the Inspector General for the U.S. Department of Education would use these findings to testify to Congress in June 1996 that accrediting agencies were "reluctant to set and enforce meaningful performance standards," and that the U.S. Department of Education "should be required to develop minimum uniform quality assurance standards, with which all recognized accrediting bodies that accredit proprietary schools must comply [and] . . . be responsible not only for formulating those standards, but also for developing and carrying out a meaningful review and verification process designed to enforce compliance with those standards" (Bloom, 1996).

In 1995, ACCSCT submitted its petition for continued recognition by the U.S. Department of Education. The U.S. Department of Education's staff analysis found that ACCSCT did not comply with 34 CFR §602.26(b)(9) that required an accrediting agency to have standards that demonstrated school "success with respect to student achievement in relation to mission, including, as appropriate, consideration of course completion, state licensing examination, and job placement" (U.S. Department of Education, 1995). The U.S. Department of Education staff analysis pointed out that ACCSCT "has historically tracked and continues to track student success" but also relied on the 1994 OIG audit that found that ACCSCT had "not developed quantitative standards to assess member schools' success with respect to student achievement." While the U.S. Department of Education determined that ACCSCT was "addressing this issue and . . . showed a willingness to meet Department criteria in this regard," ultimately the U.S. Department of

Education stated that ACCSCT needed to "define what is meant by 'reasonable' and 'acceptable' . . . [and] strengthen its compliance with the requirements of [the federal regulations]" (U.S. Department of Education, 1995).

The U.S. Department of Education continued ACCSCT's recognition, but made clear its expectation that ACCSCT establish quantitative measures as required by the 1992 amendments. From 1995 through 1998, ACCSCT continued its subjective analysis of student achievement outcomes but also continued its student achievement studies. The statistical analysis found a consistent significant correlation between program length and program completion and that "[f]or every 10 week increase in program length, graduation rates decrease by about 2 to 3.5 percentage points" (Lewis, 1996, p. 11). This led ACCSCT to conclude that program length could be useful in establishing benchmark standards for the vocational programs offered at its accredited institutions. With regard to job placement, the statistical analysis did not produce any significant correlations between student or institutional factors and the rates at which students obtained employment.

ACCSCT's petition for continued recognition would again be due in June 1998, and as of the commission's April 1998 meeting, no changes had been made to the standards of accreditation. The commission had, however, sent proposed revisions to its member institutions that included quantitative tripwires for required rates of program completion and job placement. The debate leading up to the April 1998 meeting about the use of quantitative measures included some of the issues addressed in the 1995 OIG report, among others. The OIG had found, or least interpreted, that accrediting agencies

> were reluctant to use performance data to assess the effectiveness of schools' job training programs primarily because they do not view their role as government regulators. They also expressed concerns that member schools would initiate lawsuits or simply switch to an accrediting agency having lower standards if they attempted to hold schools accountable for results. (USDE-OIG, 1995, p. 1)

In addition to these concerns, ACCSCT felt that a "one size fits all" approach would not work given the diversity of its accredited institutions and due to the socioeconomic challenges typically presented by the schools' student population, such as lower income, academic preparedness, first-generation college students, fluctuations in the job markets, and so forth. Lastly, the commission wrestled over whether institutions would lose sight of the importance of achieving maximum quality to focus solely on meeting the minimum requirements for program completion and job placement rates.

ACCSCT spent several days at that April 1998 meeting going over the comments from its member institutions, statistical analysis of program completion and job placement data, and recommendations from Dr. Morgan Lewis of the Center on Education and Training at the Ohio State University, who had conducted the statistical analysis for ACCSCT. Dr. Lewis had recommended that the commission establish a student achievement standard for program completion that would vary based upon program length. Further, he recommended that the commission use standard deviation to establish a "safe zone" for programs performing below average, requiring intervention on the commission's behalf only after a program's rate of completion fell one standard deviation below the average for all programs of comparable length. Because standard deviation measures the frequency dispersion around the mean, this would ensure that only the group of lowest-performing programs would require ACCSCT review and possible action. (In a normal bell curve, the standard deviation will capture 34% above and below the median, which leaves 16% below the standard deviation.)

The statistical analysis had shown that factors such as size of an institution's enrollment and percentage of students eligible to receive federal financial aid had a significant correlation with rates of program completion (Lewis, 1996). Also, while ACCSCT did not find statistically significant correlations between student and institutional factors and the rates of job placement, this did not mean that relationships did not exist. Anecdotally, at least, it was known that external factors did impact a school's performance as related to the job attainment of its graduates. Certainly, an institution that operated in an area with a high unemployment rate would likely have a lower rate of job placement in its programs. Again, the commission believed that by intervening only when an institution's rates fell below the standard deviation from the average (i.e., mean), many of the factors that impact a school's performance relative to student achievement would be allowed for. That is to say, schools were to be held accountable for below-average performance in their programs, but only when program performance fell significantly below average as measured by the standard deviation.

Leading up to the April 1998 meeting, ACCSCT had tried to argue to the U.S. Department of Education that its input standards such as the use of Program Advisory Committees and its standard for "reasonable" rates of program completion and job attainment should suffice to demonstrate compliance with the 1992 amendments to the Higher Education Act. However, Mark Pelesh, ACCSCT's legal counsel at the time, informed the commissioners that, based on his interaction with federal regulators, anything short of quantitative measures would put ACCSCT's continued recognition by the U.S. Department of Education in jeopardy. At that point, the debate was over, and, quite reluctantly, ACCSCT established and promulgated its student achievement standard effective July 1, 1998, requiring that for each program, an institution must "demonstrate successful student achievement" and "acceptable rates" of student graduation and employment attainment for each program offered. Acceptable rates are defined as those that are at least within one standard deviation below the mean for comparable programs, and comparability is measured primarily by program length. An important addition to the standard allowed for institutions with rates below the established benchmark to demonstrate successful student achievement "taking into account economic conditions, location, student population served, length of program, state requirements, and other external or mitigating factors reasonably related to student achievement" (ACCSCT, 1998–2006a).

As an example of how the requirements described above are set forth, ACCSCT established the following benchmark student achievement rates in 2006 based upon student achievement data collected from 2002–2004 (ACCSCT, 2006b) (see Table 6.1).

With ACCSCT's promulgation of its student achievement standard, it had closed the chapter on its history regarding the accountability-laden 1992 amendments to the Higher Education Act. At the same time, ACCSCT opened a new chapter in its use of accountability standards in a much more dynamic manner than had ever been done in the past. Once ACCSCT and its accredited institutions began to embrace the concept of benchmarking and using student achievement data as a tool for improvement, a shift began to occur in the central process of the accreditation model. Throughout its history, NATTS/ACCSCT had created a set of input driven accreditation standards that put forth minimum requirements in areas such as faculty qualifications, equipment, learning resources, finances, and so forth, with the assumption that minimum compliance with those standards would produce

TABLE 6.1
Student Achievement Rates (2002–2004)

Program Length (months)	Average Rate of Program Completion	Standard Deviation	Benchmark Rates of Program Completion
1–6	88%	11%	77%
7–11	72%	13%	59%
12–17	65%	16%	49%
18–23	62%	19%	43%
24+	55%	20%	35%

Rates of Employment Attainment		
Average Rate of Employment Attainment (all programs)	Standard Deviation	Benchmark Rates of Employment Attainment (all programs)
83%	13%	70%

positive outcomes. However, once student achievement outcomes and benchmarking became a real part of the accreditation model, those outcomes could be used to understand the interplay between input requirements and student achievement.

ACCSCT Student-Centered Model of Accreditation After 1998

Subsequent to ACCSCT's promulgation of its new student achievement standard and quantitative benchmarks, it became evident within the first year that the number of institutions under sanction for student achievement concerns decreased significantly. Before, ACCSCT had used 60 percent as a trigger to begin a process of student achievement outcomes reporting and analysis for both program completion and job placement, but the new standard only required the commission to be concerned with the statistical outliers (i.e., more than one standard deviation below the mean). So, while there had been much consternation that the use of a "bright-line" measure would increase the number of institutions on student achievement outcomes reporting, in fact the opposite occurred.

By 2002, ACCSCT's approach had been institutionalized, but its implementation had primarily defaulted to the quantitative measures, with little emphasis on qualitative factors that impacted the rates of program completion and job placement. In 1993, ACCSCT engaged in a research project to examine its student achievement standard over the span of its five-year history. This research found that the average program completion rates were going down each year, and that the standard deviation was increasing (McComis, 2003). These findings were alarming, and harkened back to one of the commission's original concerns that institutions would begin to focus on simply meeting the "standard," or minimum requirement, and that all institutions would not always be inclined to achieve maximum performance. This led to the conclusion that too much emphasis and reliance was being placed on a simple review of the numbers, both by institutions and by the commission. Ultimately, this research led to a reexamination of how ACCSCT viewed and applied its student achievement standard. This reexamination returned the organization to an original underlying premise of the student achievement requirements: that the quantitative data was really just the starting point of the analysis, and that without a qualitative understanding of the quantitative data, only a partial assessment could be accomplished.

ACCSCT started with the idea that students had to be at the center of the review paradigm, and that the accreditation input standards had to be viewed in the context of how they contributed to or detracted from the success of students. The model (see Figure 6.1) puts student success at its center, with the input and operational components of the institution serving as "spokes in the wheel" giving strength, stability, and form to the institution and bringing all of the units together at the hub or core of the institution and its ultimate mission – student success. In addition, the model calls for continuous self-evaluation and 360-degree institutional assessment and improvement to ensure that misalignment does not occur, thus helping the institution to move forward efficiently and effectively fulfilling its mission. The model represents a blended approach between quantitative methods and qualitative methods and ultimately led to a restatement of ACCSCT's mission to focus more on student success and less on accreditation as a regulatory endeavor that is simply concerned with compliance.

Many accrediting agencies and colleges continue to oppose standardized measures, arguing that simple statistics can't effectively evaluate such complex institutions. The Council for Higher Education Accreditation, which represents 3,000 colleges and universities and more than sixty accrediting organizations, told Congress in 2003 that its members "oppose any 'bright'

A Student-Centered Approach to Assessment

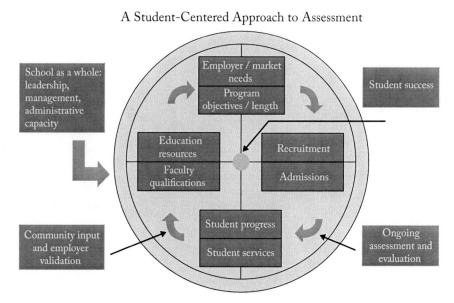

Figure 6.1 A Student-Centered Approach to Assessment

persistence-or completion-rate standard" for institutions. Such an approach, the group said, "would be ill-conceived because it ignores the obvious and enormous variety" of colleges and universities in the United States (Farrell, 2003).

ACCSCT concurs that simply using quantitative measures alone does not work, and that it will serve only to lower standards. This is why ACCSCT is an adherent of using the student-centered approach, which blends the quantitative analysis (i.e., graduation rates and employment attainment rates) with the qualitative factors that influence and impact that data. If a school demonstrates below-average rates or rates below the benchmark rates established by accrediting standards, the school must be asked why. What qualitative, institutional, or exogenous factors are impinging on student success? By using student achievement outcomes in this way, as a mechanism geared toward institutional assessment and improvement, the accreditation process becomes more meaningful and can be used as both a blueprint and a tool for success. Moreover, this process means that accreditation cannot simply rely upon mundane statistics, and that rates of graduation and employment are but one source of information in an overall assessment of institutional and student success.

As an example of this process, if ACCSCT finds that an institution has a low rate of graduation in a program, the commission will ask the following kinds of questions. Why does the institution believe that this program is low-performing, and what factors are influencing the rate? Is the program serving the needs of employers? What do employers and program advisors who represent the employment community have to say about the program? Are faculty adequately qualified (both in technical and teaching skill) to teach the program? Are there adequate resources to support the program? Does the institution have the services necessary to support student success? These kinds of questions are an important part of a student-centered process of accreditation, for they focus squarely on enhancing every opportunity for student success.

ACCSCT has changed significantly over its forty-year period history, many of these changes taking on the characteristics of the prevailing political and social movements, from President Johnson's Great Society and the era of excess in the 1980s to eras of reform and accountability in the 1990s and 2000s. ACCSCT's movement to a student-centered model of accreditation and accountability after the 1992 amendments to the Higher Education Act positioned the agency well to address the concerns of the George W. Bush administration and its agenda for greater accountability in education. Viewed through this prism, ACCSCT would again see accreditation issues come into focus and question. Just as the OIG audit for the U.S. Department of Education and the reauthorization of the Higher Education Act in 1992 had influenced accountability and accreditation in the 1990s for national accreditation and for-profit institutions, another OIG audit and Higher Education Act reauthorization would do the same in the 2000s. In the 2000s, however, ACCSCT's use of quantitative student achievement performance outcomes would put the agency and other national accrediting agencies in a position to show the higher education community the merits of this approach.

Accountability in the New Millennium

The Bush administration released its strategic plan for improving higher education in 2002. The plan, which was prepared for reauthorization of the Higher Education Act, emphasized institutional accountability and transparency, asserting that all colleges should be held accountable for their effectiveness in retaining students and graduating them "in a timely fashion"

(Bush, 2001, p. 61). Reflecting a growing concern that the United States could become less competitive in global markets if it did not keep pace with the increasing economic demand for highly skilled professionals, the plan called for colleges to systematically assess and report on their performance. The administration described this as necessary to address critical workforce needs and to justify the $70 billion in federal student aid and direct support of postsecondary education. Over the next seven years, the role and effectiveness of accreditation in quality assurance would again be explored through higher education act reauthorization, various U.S. Department of Education initiatives, and a second OIG audit. Accreditation's role in leading higher education to focus more on student achievement became central to these discussions with national accrediting agencies prepared to show their model of quality assurance was student-centered.

The Bush administration's plan was motivated, in part, by evidence of a widening achievement gap among postsecondary students, and evidence that lower income and non-traditional students were being underserved by higher education (Carey, 2004). A 2002 report by the National Center of Education Statistics (NCES) tracked a representative sample of over 10,000 students who enrolled for the first time in a four-year institution in fall 1995 and found that only six out of ten graduated with a degree within six years (Muraskin & Lee, 2004). A disproportionately high number of the students who did not graduate were low-income and minority students (Muraskin & Lee, 2004). The six-year completion rate for African-American students and Latinos in 2002 was only about 46 percent (Lumina, 2005). Of all students enrolled in community colleges in 1995–1996, only 26 percent of African-Americans and 29 percent of Hispanic students attained a certificate or degree within six years, compared with 38 percent of white students and 39 percent of Asian students (Lumina, 2005). The eventual impact on the economy of an underserved student population and prolonged *time to workforce* strengthened the administration's arguments for greater accountability.

Some economists supported the Bush administration's position complaining that higher education markets behaved inefficiently when information on academic quality was either imperfect or unavailable. Students, who needed to know about how a college would provide advantages in job placement, successful admission to graduate school, and the income of graduates were forced to rely on directories, guidebooks, and rankings that did not address an institution's actual performance in helping students learn and succeed (Dill & Soo, 2004). Guidebook information alone could not assist students in reaching college decisions that were aligned with their personal education and career goals (Carey, 2004). This view of students as "consumers" has historically been controversial (Blaum, 2005; Swagler, 1978).

Scarce information on the performance of higher education institutions also caused institutions themselves to misallocate resources. Institutions focused on enhancing their reputations were inclined to invest in research and amenities that would attract high-ability students instead of in resources intended to improve teaching and learning. Unless faculty were held accountable for performance, they focused on academic individuality rather than on collaborative review of curriculum, teaching methods, and learning objectives that would ensure coherent and purposeful instruction. Economists suggested that making student achievement information public would motivate faculty to coordinate efforts toward improving program quality and cause more resources to be directed into the classroom (Dill & Soo, 2004). The academy acknowledged that a lack of coordinated effort on the part of faculty could affect quality (Bennett, 2007; Rosovsky & Ameer, 1998).

By the time the administration's strategic plan was released in 2002, the for-profit sector of education had already embraced measuring student achievement as part of an accountability-based model of education. The for-profits tended to emphasize educational outputs—student satisfaction, retention rates, completion rates, and placement rates—while the non-profits continued to place a higher value on inputs: admissions selectivity, faculty credentials, and extracurricular programs and activities (Ruch, 2001). This emphasis was reinforced by accreditation standards that required employer advisory committees to provide regular feedback on program marketability, curriculum development, technology, equipment, and placement services (ACCSCT, 1998–2006a). For-profit education also incorporated a traditional management model, in which managers who were given significant decision making authority were also held accountable for outcomes. There was an emphasis on tight supervision and market responsiveness, which required an institution to adapt rapidly, updating curricula continuously and adjusting program offerings to accord with market demand (Ruch, 2001).

It is unclear how much influence this for-profit model had on the development of the Bush administration's plan, but by 2002, for-profit education had gained the attention of the higher education community, policymakers, and certain economists. For-profit colleges and universities were successful because they had responded, with greater attention to management, to the evolution of the knowledge-based economy, the expansion of the adult education market, and improvements in technology (Ruch, 2001). The ability of the for-profit sector to align with these market changes, to meet consumer expectations for employability, and to respond to the demand for value-added measurement were important factors in its success (Ruch, 2001).

While advocates for accountability and better consumer information on institutional performance believed that it would improve the efficiency of higher education markets and the quality of education, deeper analysis suggested that the administration was really calling for a cultural transformation within the academy that would focus teaching and learning on students and would hold institutions accountable for successful student achievement.

The *No Child Left Behind Act* (*NCLB*), signed into law in January 2002, was a significant event for higher education because the principles of accountability and student achievement upon which the act was based also became the cornerstone of the administration's strategic plan for higher education (Bush, 2002, p. 2) The Executive Summary of the *NCLB* Act introduces its priorities with the following quotation:

> The priorities that follow are based on the fundamental notion that an enterprise works best when responsibility is placed closest to the most important activity of the enterprise, when those responsible are given greatest latitude and support and when those responsible are held accountable for producing results. This education blueprint will: increase accountability for student performance: States, districts and schools that improve achievement will be rewarded. Failure will be sanctioned. (Bush, 2002, p. 2)

These themes of accountability for student performance and results are repeated in the higher education plan. Strategic Objective 5.2 of the plan is intended to "[s]trengthen the accountability of postsecondary institutions"; it describes the U.S. Department of Education's intention to integrate measures of student achievement into state accountability systems for higher education, and to use them in evaluating postsecondary institutions (Bush, 2001, p. 61).

Similarities between the administration's plan and *NCLB* also prompted anxious discussions about whether the U.S. Department of Education intended to expand its oversight of higher education. The higher education community became immediately concerned that the administration would attempt to link a college's eligibility to award federal student aid to its success at retaining and graduating students. Some colleges and universities argued that they should not be penalized for educating large numbers of low-income students, part-time students, and older students—all considered to be at high risk of dropping out (Burd, 2002). Higher education officials and lobbyists asserted that the quality of higher education was the responsibility of institutions and accrediting agencies, and that the role of the federal government should be limited to ensuring that colleges properly manage taxpayer dollars appropriated to student aid programs (Burd, 2002).

The debate over the proper federal role in higher education dominated discussions of reauthorization of the higher education act as well. Many higher education organizations took the position that the federal government should not "delve into issues of institutional quality" (Burd, 2002). Others recognized that federal leadership was necessary in areas of global economic competition, and to support higher levels of success in postsecondary education to that end. The search for a proper balance between institutional autonomy and government intervention became a central part of the debate in higher education accountability. In a 2005 article, Paul Lingenfelter, executive director of the State Higher Education Officers (SHEEO), noted that accountability for improved performance in higher education was in demand and urged policymakers to consider carefully what accountability policies would help improve achievement and quality without excessive regulation and centralization of educational decision making (Lingenfelter & Lenth, 2005).

Lingenfelter invited a reassessment of federal, state, and institutional roles, urging the federal government to give the states and institutions a national data framework to help states and institutions identify problems with and improve transfer, persistence, and graduation rates. Institutions, for their part, were encouraged to be more forthright and explicit about expectations and more systematic about assessment, and to disclose the results of assessments and trends in learning in order to improve public confidence in higher education. Lingenfelter cautioned against minimum standards of student achievement, however, fearing that such standards would impede academic freedom, flexibility, and openness to innovation (Lingenfelter & Lenth, 2005).

Regional accrediting organizations shared this concern. In testimony before the U.S. Department of Education in November 2006, Belle

Wheelan of the Southern Association of Colleges and Schools warned that then existing federal regulations on student achievement were "cookie-cutter" and needed to allow flexibility to encourage institutions, through accrediting commission initiatives, to focus on student learning. She asked, "[h]ow can accrediting commissions address fundamental issues related to the transformation of higher education when current federal regulations accept only cookie-cutter responses?" (U.S. Department of Education, 2006).

Early conversations around the administration's strategic plan and higher education act reauthorization focused on the role of the federal government, states, and institutions in the accountability question. The role that accreditation would play in the higher education transformation envisioned by the administration was unclear. Accreditation as a model of quality assurance was not well understood by Congress. Advocates of higher education reform saw accreditation as part of the problem, viewing it as lacking in accountability and quality, secretive and guildlike (Leef & Burris, 2002). Others, including House Education and Labor Committee member Tom Petri (D-WI), asserted that the government's reliance on accreditation as a gatekeeper for access to federal student aid was misplaced (H.R. 4283, 2004). The spectrum of suggested reforms to accreditation ranged from modest changes requiring a greater focus on accountability and student achievement to the most extreme position: creating a new system of quality assurance not involving accreditation at all (Leef & Burris, 2002). Although much of the criticism of accreditation was targeted at the six regional accrediting organizations, many regarded the accrediting community as homogeneous and therefore failed to distinguish different accreditation models. This was frustrating to the national accrediting organizations, whose student outcomes–focused model of accreditation seemed consistent with the goals of the administration's plan but was being overlooked even as Senate hearings on HEA reauthorization were taking place.

One outspoken organization on the accreditation issue was the American Council of Trustees and Alumni (ACTA) whose chair, Dr. Jerry Martin, testified before the Senate Health, Education, Labor and Pensions (HELP) Committee in February 2004. Martin testified that "accreditors have great power, but they do not assure quality, [that] accreditation standards have little to do with learning and that accreditors' performance was a persistent failure" (Council for Higher Education Accreditation, 2004, p. 39). He argued for severing the linkage between federal student aid eligibility and accreditation, favoring instead a collaborative system between federal and state governments in which the states would be responsible for establishing and enforcing performance measures and the federal government would assure that institutions properly carried out their fiduciary responsibilities for administering federal student aid programs. Ultimately, in Dr. Martin's view, college and university trustees should play the chief role in strengthening academic standards at their own institutions (Council for Higher Education Accreditation, 2004).

Steve Crow, executive director of the Higher Learning Commission, expressed a different view. He characterized institutional quality, student learning, and transparency as new concerns of the present reauthorization. He stressed that reforms must seek to preserve the unique missions and discretion of institutions (Crow, 2004). A consensus forming within the traditional higher education community suggested that "modest" reforms to accreditation would achieve the country's policy goals. This position was also articulated by the Council on Higher Education Accreditation (CHEA) and other higher education organizations at the time.

While some senators on the HELP Committee seemed to agree with that position, they seemed to have little confidence in accreditation. Senator Lamar Alexander (R-TN) stressed that federal law directs accreditation to determine "sufficient quality"—described as a correctly minimal standard— to receive federal support, reinforcing the view that we should look to higher education institutions themselves to be accountable for student learning and achievement. Senator Sessions (R-AL) was concerned about a perceived lack of due process in recent accreditation decisions affecting institutions in his state. Hillary Rodham Clinton (D-NY) spoke against regulation that would interfere with institutional autonomy and independence, which she regarded as "precious" (Council for Higher Education Accreditation, 2004).

National accreditation and nationally accredited institutions played a larger role in discussions in the House, where Chairman Howard "Buck" McKeon (R-CA) had introduced H.R. 4283, known as the *College Access and Opportunity Act of 2004*, which contained provisions aimed at improving institutional accountability. The bill would have required institutions to provide students with a summary of student outcomes for full-time undergraduate students, including completion or graduation rates, information related to transfer students, and any other student outcome data related to the institution's educational mission and goals. (Section 485(L)(i) and (ii) p. 138).

H.R. 4283 was also intended to hold accrediting agencies accountable by requiring them to make more information about their standards and processes public. On June 22, 2004, the House Subcommittee on 21st Century Competitiveness heard testimony on three main issues: What more could accrediting agencies do to ensure quality? Should there be more independence in the accreditation process? Should the Congress do more to require specific standards for accrediting agencies? Chairman McKeon indicated at the outset that he continued to support the basic role of accreditation as the means to assure quality in higher education, but also that he wanted provisions in the legislation that would strengthen accountability and provide more transparency to empower consumers (H.R. 4283, 2004).

Dr. Arthur Keiser, chancellor of the Keiser Collegiate System and chair of the Accrediting Commission of Career Schools and Colleges of Technology (ACCSCT), testified before the subcommittee on the topic "Does Accreditation Provide Students and Parents Accountability and Quality?" Dr. Keiser expressed his view that accreditation provided quality assurance for students and shared the committee's interest in strengthening that role through passage of the bill's provisions on accreditation. He noted that ACCSCT and other national accrediting organizations had adopted and refined a model of accreditation that required institutions to calculate graduation and job placement rates, and to achieve certain benchmarks. He asserted that all accrediting agencies should be capable of collecting and reviewing such data as a way of strengthening programs and holding them accountable for meeting objectives, as they defined them (H.R. 4283, 2004).

Dr. Keiser's positions relative to accountability and student achievement differed from the positions of traditional higher education and accreditation at the time by signaling a need for accreditation to play a more significant role in requiring the systematic evaluation of student achievement. This would not have presented a significant change for national accrediting agencies that had been using quantitative measures of student achievement as part of the accreditation process since 1998. Regional accrediting organizations and higher education associations, however, were opposed to additional federal regulation, particularly if it mandated a single approach to measuring institutional effectiveness. They worried that one size fits all approaches to accountability would seriously undermine the autonomy of institutions and the diversity of U.S. higher education.

Although not raised as a topic during the reauthorization hearings in 2004, the *Final Audit Report of the Accrediting Agency Evaluation Unit's Review of Selected Accrediting Agency Standards and Procedures*, issued in July 2003, was a reminder that Congress had been concerned about accountability and student achievement since 1992. The purpose of this OIG audit was to ensure that the U.S. Department of Education required recognized accrediting agencies to establish standards addressing educational institutions' success with respect to student achievement, to continuously monitor institutions' compliance with the standards, and to take consistent enforcement action when institutions were not in compliance with the standards. The regulations at 34 CFR §602.16(a)(1)(i) stated that agencies must have an accreditation standard addressing success with respect to student achievement in relation to the institution's mission, including—*as appropriate*—consideration of course completion, state licensing examination, and job placement rates. This regulation was interpreted in the preamble to the 1994 final regulations and the 1999 proposed rules as being applicable to programs that provided vocational education.

The OIG found that regional and national accrediting agencies had been treated differently by the U.S. Department of Education, which did not require regional accrediting agencies to establish quantitative student achievement standards for institutions that offered vocational education programs. The OIG asserted that the regulation had been intended to apply to all vocational programs, regardless of accrediting agency, and reasoned that students enrolled in vocational training programs had the same expectation of obtaining gainful employment whether the institution offering the program was accredited by a regional or national accrediting agency. Thus, the OIG concluded that regional and national accrediting agencies should be held to the same requirements of quantitative standards for student achievement. Ultimately, the OIG recommended that the U.S. Department of Education develop a reauthorization proposal to clarify and require that every accrediting agency establish quantitative standards for student achievement for vocational programs (USDE-OIG, 2003).

The OIG report on accreditation and the testimony of the national accrediting commissions before the two key congressional committees provided an opening for national accrediting organizations to share their ten-year experience with accountability and student achievement at a time when the administration was most interested in reform. The national accrediting agencies thus positioned themselves as willing partners in higher education and accreditation reform as traditional higher education and regional accrediting agencies continued to push for the *status quo*. With the 2004 election and a new majority in Congress the following year, the administration, under Secretary of Education Margaret Spellings, began an aggressive push toward realizing the administration's strategic plan through the establishment of the Commission on the Future of Higher Education (the Spellings Commission). Representatives of the for-profit sector and national accreditation served as resources to the secretary during this time, bringing a fresh perspective on education that fit well with the secretary's own views and the administration's concerns about workforce preparation and global competitiveness.

In September 2006, the Spellings Commission released a report entitled *A Test of Leadership: Charting the Future of U.S. Higher Education*. The report was compiled from the notes of stakeholder hearings that began in 2005 on topics discussed in the Bush administration's strategic plan: accountability, affordability, accessibility, quality, and innovation in higher education. In establishing a framework for the commission's recommendations, the report described U.S. higher education as follows:

> What we have learned over the last year makes clear that higher education has become what, in the business world, would be called a mature enterprise: increasingly risk-averse, at times self-satisfied, and uniquely expensive. It is an enterprise that has yet to address the fundamental issues of how academic programs and institutions must be transformed to serve the changing educational needs of a knowledge economy. It has yet to successfully confront the impact of globalization, rapidly evolving technologies, an increasingly diverse and aging population and an evolving marketplace characterized by new needs and paradigms. (U.S. Department of Education, 2006, p. xii)

The Spellings Commission report suggested that higher education would have to change from a system primarily based on reputation to one based on performance in order to serve this evolving marketplace and new paradigm. The report states:

> We urge the creation of a robust culture of accountability and transparency throughout higher education. Every one of our goals, from improving access and affordability to enhancing quality and innovation, will be more easily

achieved if higher education institutions embrace and implement serious accountability measures. (U.S. Department of Education, 2006, p. 21)

While focused more broadly on higher education reform, the Spellings Commission as a whole also called for changes to accreditation that some members of the commission nevertheless regarded as an impediment to innovation. In the commission's view, accreditation needed to focus less on process, inputs, and governance and more on "bottom-line results" for learning, costs, and quality, and to become more transparent to address the growing demand for increased accountability.

In spite of the Spellings Commission's bleak view of accreditation, the secretary seemed to recognize that accreditation could be a catalyst for change because its role as a gatekeeper for federal student aid gave the U.S. Department of Education regulatory authority and influence over accreditation. Reforming accreditation quickly became a central focus of Secretary Spellings's strategy for implementing the Spellings Commission's recommendations. In a multi-faceted approach, the secretary sought to build consensus around the idea of accreditation reform. In March 2006, the U.S. Department of Education hosted a round table discussion on accreditation. A symposium on the Futures Commission report was held in March 2007 followed by a series of regional meetings. The secretary conducted negotiated rulemaking on the recognition criteria for accrediting agencies in 34 CFR Section 602 *et seq.*, despite not having a reauthorized higher education act, and made sympathetic appointments to the National Advisory Committee on Institutional Quality and Integrity, the committee responsible for advising her on higher education policy and making recommendations for the recognition of accrediting agencies.

The first event, the Accreditation Roundtable, focused on how accreditation should respond to changes in the higher education environment including: the changing structure and delivery of higher education, distance learning, cost effectiveness, and globalization. The secretary's message—that accreditation needed to change—was made clear through the questions posed to round table participants, such as the following: How can accreditation assure the government and the public that higher education institutions and programs are effective in achieving results, especially student learning outcomes? What is the relationship between accreditation and student accountability mechanisms? (See chapter Appendix B.). Representatives of the national accrediting agencies attended these events and shared information about their outcomes assessment models. The employment community was also represented and shared a perspective on accountability that was closely aligned with the national accreditation model.

Accreditation was an important topic during a symposium held one year later, in March 2007, entitled *A Test of Leadership: Committing to Advance Postsecondary Education for All Americans*, sponsored by the U.S. Department of Education. One of the discussion groups was organized around how accreditation should be reformed to emphasize student achievement and to be more transparent. Participants were asked to offer ideas for how to increase public awareness and understanding of accreditation through greater transparency, how to create collective ownership at the institutional level for using student learning outcomes as a measure of institutional effectiveness, how to develop and pilot the use of transparent measures of core learning outcomes to facilitate comparisons across similar institutions, how to align accreditor, state, and federal requirements for measuring and reporting student learning outcomes and processes to reduce redundancy in reporting, and how to design a process for developing a national qualifications framework similar to that recommended by SHEEO.

Reactions to the Roundtable and Symposium discussions surrounding accreditation's role in student achievement were mixed. Some regionally accredited colleges and universities, such as the Pennsylvania State System and James Madison University, already had systems for collecting data on student performance (Lederman, 2008). With that in mind, higher education officials argued that institutions should develop their own models of assessing student achievement, aligning with institutional mission and opposing any system imposed by accreditation or government regulation. Common measures that were forced on institutions by the U.S. Department of Education or accrediting organizations could lead to oversimplification and "minimum standards" that could have an adverse impact on institutional performance (Lederman, 2008).

Few, if any, in higher education supported a one size fits all approach, and Secretary Spellings and her staff stated on numerous occasions that one size fits all was not the goal. Thus the challenge for educators was to define a system of assessing student achievement that would be flexible enough to account for the vast differences in higher education institutions and still give student–consumers relevant and comparable information to assist with their decision making. Many believed that this was not an appropriate role for accreditation or the federal government. Those who favored reform, including the national accrediting organizations, believed that the Spellings initiatives were causing reflection that could lead to a positive result.

Transparency in the accreditation process was another important theme of the Roundtable and Symposium discussions. Should accrediting commissions be required to disclose to the public more information about accreditation standards and processes and individual accreditation decisions? Views on this topic varied widely, the most conservative position being that disclosure would smother the trust and collegiality between an accrediting agency and its institutions and provide little in the way of meaningful information to students to help them in their decision making (Eaton, Fryshman, Hope, Scanlon, & Crow, 2005). Some people stressed the need for balancing the public role of accrediting agencies as gatekeepers to federal student aid and the need for collegiality and candor in the relationships of accrediting organizations and their institutions. On this topic, Steve Crow, the executive director of the Higher Learning Commission of the North Central Association, signaled a need for more openness.

> To some people the credibility of accreditation is as suspect as the success of our colleges and universities in graduating well-educated students. Policymakers, students, parents and employers have started to question the effectiveness of third party quality assurance, especially quality assurance grounded on judgments of peers applying standards created by peers . . . [w]e cloak ourselves in confidentiality while trying to explain what we do and why, [and] the inquirers only wonder what we know that is so important that we will not talk about it. (Eaton, Fryshman, Hope, Scanlon, & Crow, 2005)

By the time the symposium took place in March 2007, the secretary had already announced that she intended to include the criteria for recognition of accrediting agencies set forth under 34 CFR §602 *et seq.* as a topic in negotiated rulemaking. This was a controversial decision, because the rulemaking was to take place without a reauthorized act; many in higher education—and in Congress—questioned Spellings's authority to do so. The secretary, frustrated that Congress had not reauthorized the statute in a timely manner—the statute should have been reauthorized in 2003, but was extended several times by Congress—and feeling a duty to push for reform, went forward with the rulemaking, although, at the behest of the HELP Committee, she did not propose new regulations after the negotiations concluded. Spellings's expressed intent in conducting the rulemaking was, among other issues, to ensure that the now $80 billion dollar federal education budget was spent on quality programs. Many were suspicious about the secretary's intent, believing that "the Department [of Education] was trying to impose a new agenda on accrediting agencies" (Lederman, 2007). This resulted in a strong lobbying effort to limit the secretary's authority in regulating accrediting agencies' standards on student achievement. As with the Roundtable and Symposium, the fact that the national accrediting organizations were already using quantitative outcomes assessment models figured prominently in the negotiations.

The U.S. Department of Education presented negotiators with an issue paper that characterized its position on student achievement on the first day of the negotiation. The issue paper was interesting for a number of reasons. First, it implied that the assessment models that were being used by many of the recognized accrediting commissions did not go far enough to ensure quality. Second, the U.S. Department of Education's reference to the adequacy of student academic achievement signaled its expectation that acceptable accreditation standards would have to include benchmarks or minimum performance standards for institutions or programs. The federal negotiators indicated that it was the U.S. Department of Education's intention to resolve its own inconsistent enforcement of the regulations relative to student achievement among recognized accrediting organizations, a reference to the 2003 OIG findings and report.

A number of nationally and regionally accredited for-profit institutions were represented in this session of negotiated rulemaking, along with two national institutional accrediting agencies and two specialized agencies. The debate was not dissimilar from those that occurred during the reauthorization hearings in 2004. The regional accrediting organizations sought to preserve the assessment models already within their standards and spoke against the imposition of quantitative measures that intruded on academic decision making. They also argued that quantitative measures were impractical given the diversity of mission among institutions with regional accreditation, and given that regional accreditors did not have a process for approving individual programs and did not have the technology for benchmarking. Community college representatives weighed in near the end of the negotiation, opining that accountability for student achievement outcomes would conflict with their mission of broad access for students. There was skepticism that using quantitative measures for assessing student achievement would actually make accreditation a more effective tool, and serious concern over an expanded federal role in academic decision making through control of accreditation.

National institutional accrediting organizations, such as ACCSCT and the Accrediting Council of Continuing Education and Training, that had already adopted quantitative measures of student achievement, as described earlier in this chapter, saw the value in having done so. Holding institutions accountable for performance had created a student-centered culture within the for-profit community and had improved the quality of education. These agencies advocated for regulations that would require accrediting commissions to incorporate quantitative measures of student achievement in standards, even as part of broader, already existing accreditation processes for assessing institutional effectiveness. An important goal for the national accrediting organizations was also to ensure that any new recognition criteria would set clear expectations with regard to student achievement, and that they would be applied consistently to all recognized institutional accrediting agencies and institutions with comparable missions and programs. (Through appointments to NACIQI that included some representatives of the for-profit sector, and advocates for reform such as Ann Neal [ACTA], secretary Spellings attempted to ensure that NACIQI would place a greater emphasis on accountability and student achievement in the recognition process.)

The wide gap in the positions of the negotiators on the question of student achievement began to narrow as the negotiation progressed and the representatives of accreditation began to gain a better understanding of the challenges different accrediting agencies faced. While differences of opinion continued throughout the negotiation, and persist even today, negotiators began to find some common ground. Their views were reflected in the last version of the student achievement language proposed by the negotiators, even though consensus was not reached and the language was never adopted (see chapter Appendix C).

This middle ground reflected certain understandings that evolved during the negotiation: institutions should be held accountable for and engaged in ways of determining successful student learning and achievement. Accreditation does have a role in institutional accountability, but accreditation standards should respect the unique missions of institutions and the diversity of higher education. Institutions should have the flexibility to adopt and use assessment models that are well suited to mission. Accreditation should continue to balance its gatekeeping role (for institutional access to federal student aid) with its traditional role of supporting the continuous improvement of institutions and programs. Quantitative benchmarks for both completion and job placement should be part of an assessment model for programs with a vocational objective. The U.S. Department of Education should not set minimum quantitative standards, whether through the recognition process for accrediting agencies or directly for institutions by making federal student aid dependent upon institutions meeting a minimum quantitative standard.

In addition, the nonfederal negotiators realized that there were indeed differences in the way the recognition criteria had been applied to regional and national institutional accrediting agencies. The U.S. Department of Education's push for quantitative standards of student achievement had actually begun in 1992, not 2007, and its different treatment of national accreditation went well beyond the application of the student achievement criteria. National agencies had been required to evaluate the quality of and separately approve individual programs within accredited institutions, to have quantitative student achievement standards for programs with a vocational objective. Regional accrediting agencies were not subject to these same requirements, even though many of their institutions were also for-profit colleges. Perhaps not having anticipated the slippery slope that led to the requirement of quantitative standards, regional accreditors did not object during the early 1990s as the national accreditors were held to these strict requirements by the U.S. Department of Education. Regional accreditors and higher education associations perceived the U.S. Department of Education's attempt to enforce them more broadly after 2002 as a bold new intrusion into institutional autonomy and academic decision making (Eaton, 2008).

Accrediting agency representatives left the negotiating table with some appreciation for their different experiences and the divergent opinions those experiences had produced. The agencies also came to understand the work other accrediting agencies were doing within their own sectors on assessment and accountability, recognizing that their processes and standards could be improved by being open to the assessment tools used by other agencies. Accreditors also gained a better understanding of the challenges to accreditation associated with the changing economy, changing priorities for education, and new expectations of accreditation. The identity of accreditation as a policy force in higher education also became an interesting question. Could accreditation agencies, long believed to be a product of their membership, sustain an independent identity from their institutions? Should accreditation have an independent voice in higher education policy? Are the interests of accreditation and institutions perfectly aligned, especially on the question of student achievement? Who has the primary responsibility for setting standards of student achievement—accrediting agencies, or institutions? Those questions became important as discussions on legislative language on student achievement within HEA reauthorization resumed in fall 2007.

For the moment, a fragile compromise among higher education associations and recognized accrediting agencies has produced student achievement language in the section of the reauthorized HEA that pertains to the recognition of accrediting agencies. That language, through rules of construction, preserves for institutions and accrediting agencies the roles they have traditionally played in setting standards of student achievement. The statute also restricts the authority of the U.S. Department of Education to regulate accrediting agencies in certain areas, including student achievement.

Arguably, neither the HEA nor the rulemaking to follow will change the higher education paradigm in ways the Bush administration envisioned in its original plan, but there is evidence that accrediting agencies and institutions are moving beyond the status quo—if not by setting quantitative student achievement benchmarks as the national accrediting agencies have done, then by providing a framework for research, further discussion, and resources for institutions to focus on performance. At the Annual Conference of the Higher Learning Commission in April 2008, for example, there were nearly fifty sessions devoted to the assessment of student learning. Similarly, other regional accreditors and CHEA have held workshops for institutions on the topic of assessment, and several associations have developed assessment instruments that are being piloted in various colleges and universities. These initiatives suggest that the academy has moved beyond what was a contentious debate about change toward actual reforms that will bring about greater accountability (Fryshman, 2007). National accreditation will continue to inform the education community's accountability efforts and will continue to serve as an important resource and example, showing the value of helping institutions become more purposeful in their educational practices, and helping students become more intentional learners.

References

Accrediting Commission of Career Schools and Colleges of Technology. (1998–2006a). *Section VII (C)(2)(b), Substantive Standards, Standards of Accreditation*. Arlington, VA: Author.

Accrediting Commission of Career Schools and Colleges of Technology. (2006b). *Accreditation Alert!—Standards of Accreditation*. Retrieved February 15, 2006, from www.accsc.org/Content/Accreditation/StandardsofAccreditation/Accreditation Alerts/Archive/2006/021506%20alert%20with%20header.pdf.

Accreditation Institutional Eligibility (AIE). (1969). *Summary of the application of the Accrediting Commission of the National Association of Trade and Technical Schools for recognition as a nationally recognized accrediting agency.* Washington, DC: Author.

Baxandall, L., & Cooney, M. (1983). *NATTS: The first generation*. Oshkosh, WI: The Baxandall Company.

Bell, T. H. (1986). Education policy development in the Reagan administration. *Phi Delta Kappan, 67*(7), 487–493.

Bennett, J. B. (2007). Engaged, but not heroic, academic leadership. *Academic Leadership*. Retrieved August 27, 2008, from www.academicleadership.org/leader_action_tips/Engaged_But_Not_Heroic_Academic_Leadership.shtml.

Blaum, P. (2005). College students have evolved from clients to consumers. *Penn State Live*. Retrieved May 16, 2008 from http://live.psu.edu/story/12334.

Bloom, T. R. (1996). *Statement before the subcommittee on human resources and intergovernmental relations*. Office of Inspector General: Washington, DC. Retrieved August 27, 2008, from http://www.ed.gov/about/offices/list/oig/auditrpts/gatetst.html.

Burd, S. (2002, September 20). Accountability or meddling? Bush administration's proposals reveal growing divide between college groups and U.S. Education Department. *The Chronicle of Higher Education*, p. A23.

Bush, G. W. (2001). *Strategic Goal 5: Enhance the quality of and access to postsecondary and adult education*. U.S. Department of Education Strategic Plan 2002–2007. Jessup, MD: ED Pubs.

Bush, G. W. (2002). Executive Summary. *No Child Left Behind*. Washington, DC: Author.

Carey, K. (2004). *A matter of degrees: Improving graduation rates in four-year colleges and universities*. Washington, DC: The Education Trust.

Council for Higher Education Accreditation. (2004). U.S. Senate hearings on accreditation, February 26, 2004: Senators have questions, but dismiss "delinkage." Washington, DC: Council for Higher Education Accreditation.

Crow, S. (2004). *Higher education accreditation: How can the system better ensure quality and accountability? Testimony of Dr. Steven D. Crow, U.S. Senate Committee on*

Health, Education, Labor and Pensions. Retrieved August 28, 2008, from http://help.senate.gov/Hearings/2004_02_26/2004_02_26.html.

Dill, D. D., & Soo, M. (2004). *Transparency and quality in higher education markets.* Chapel Hill: The University of North Carolina at Chapel Hill Public Policy for Academic Quality Research Program.

Eaton, J., Fryshman, B., Hope, S., Scanlon, E., & Crow, S. (2005). Disclosure and damage: Can accreditation provide one without the other? *Change, 37*(3), 35–41.

Eaton, J. (2008, March 24). The future of accreditation? *Inside Higher Ed.* Retrieved August 28, 2008, from www.insidehighered.com/views/2008/03/24/eaton.

Fallis, G. (2004). *The mission of the university.* Retrieved July 22, 2008, from www.cou.on.ca/content/objects/The%20Mission%20V3.pdf.

Farrell, E. F. (2003, August 15). A common yardstick? *The Chronicle of Higher Education,* p. A25.

Fryshman, B. (2007, August 15). Score one for the secretary. *Inside Higher Ed.* Retrieved August, 15, 2007, from www.insidehighered.com/views/2007/08/15/fryshman.

H.R. 4283, The college access and opportunity act: Does accreditation provide students and parents accountability and quality? H.R. 4283 Cong. (June 22, 2004).

Kempfer, H., & Kempfer, H. (1966). *Proceedings: 2nd annual convention of the National Association of Trade and Technical Schools.* Washington, DC: Batt, Bates & Co.

Lederman, D. (2007, March 28). Drawing a hard line. *Inside Higher Ed.* Retrieved March 28, 2007, from www.insidehighered.com/news/2007/03/28/accredit.

Lederman, D. (2008, June 30). Foreseeing the future of accreditation. *Inside Higher Ed.* Retrieved June 30, 2008, from www.insidehighered.com/news/2008/06/30/accredit.

Leef, G. C., & Burris, R. D. (2002). *Can college accreditation live up to its promise?* Washington, DC: American Council of Trustees and Alumni.

Lewis, M. (1996). *Student outcomes at private, accredited career schools and colleges of technology: An analysis of annual report data for the school years 1990–1994.* Columbus: The Center on Education and Training at the Ohio State University.

Lingenfelter, P. E., & Lenth, C. S. (2005). What should reauthorization be about? *Change, 37*(3), 12–19.

Lumina Foundation for Education. (2005). *Achieving the dream: Community colleges are focus of broad initiative.* Retrieved July 25, 2008, from www.luminafoundation.org/newsroom/Jan2005/AtD.html.

McComis, M. (2003). *Student achievement outcomes research project.* Arlington, VA: Accrediting Commission of Career Schools and Colleges of Technology.

Millard, R. (1983). Accreditation. In J. R. Warren (Ed.), *Meeting the new demand for standards: New directions for higher education* (pp. 9–28). San Francisco, CA: Jossey-Bass.

Muraskin, L., & Lee, J. (2004). *Raising the graduation rates of low-income college students.* Washington, DC: The Pell Institute for the Study of Opportunity in Higher Education.

National Association of Trade and Technical Schools (NATTS), Accrediting Commission of Trade and Technical Schools (ACTTS), Accrediting Commission of Career Schools and Colleges of Technology (ACCSCT) (1966–2008). *Membership directory.* Arlington, VA: Author.

National Association of Trade and Technical Schools. (1990). *Standards of accreditation.* Arlington, VA: Author.

National Commission on Excellence in Education (NCEE). (1983). *A nation at risk.* Washington, DC: Author.

Public regional hearing for negotiated rulemaking before the U.S. Department of Education, Office of Postsecondary Education, U.S. Department of Education, 13 (2008). Retrieved August 28, 2008, from www.ed.gov/policy/highered/reg/hearulemaking/hea08/transcript-10-08-08.pdf.

Rosovsky, H., & Ameer, I. L. (1998). A neglected topic: Professional conduct of college and university teachers. In W. G. Bowen & H. T. Shapiro (Eds.), *Universities and their leadership* (pp. 136). Princeton, NJ: Princeton University Press.

Ruch, R. S. (2001). Foreword and confessions of a for-profit dean. In G. Kelly (Ed.), *Higher Ed, Inc.: The rise of the for-profit university* (pp. x, 7). Baltimore: The Johns Hopkins University Press.

Swagler, R. M. (1978). Students as consumers of postsecondary education: A framework for analysis. *The Journal of Consumer Affairs, 12*(1), 126–134.

Swenson, C., Warren, D., & Boggs, G. (2005). Point/counterpoint. *Change, 37*(3), 20–27.

Tolbert, J. (1979). *The role of private trade and technical school in a comprehensive human development system: Implications for research and development, Occasional paper #53.* Columbus: The National Center for Research in Vocational Education, The Ohio State University.

U.S. Department of Education. (2006). *A test of leadership: Charting the future of U.S. higher education. A report of the commission appointed by Secretary of Education Margaret Spellings.* Jessup, MD: ED Pubs.

U.S. Department of Education, Office of the Inspector General. (1995). *Staff analysis of ACCSCT petition for recognition.* Washington, DC: ED Pubs.

U.S. Department of Education, Office of Inspector General. (2003). *Office of Postsecondary Education, Accrediting Agency Evaluation Unit's Review of Selected Accrediting Agency Standards and Procedures: Final Audit Report ED-OIG/A09-C0014.* Washington, DC: ED Pubs.

U.S. Senate, Permanent Subcommittee on Investigations of the Committee on Governmental Affairs (1991). *Abuses in federal student aid programs.* Washington, DC: U.S. Senate.

Endnotes

¹ Subsequent to the writing of this chapter, the Accrediting Commission of Career Schools and Colleges of Technology (ACCSCT) changed its name to the Accrediting Commission of Career Schools and Colleges (ACCSC).

7

A GLOBAL PERSPECTIVE ON FOR-PROFIT HIGHER EDUCATION

Kevin Kinser

For-profit higher education presents a confusing case for global analysis. In most countries, commercially oriented institutions form the bulk of the expanding private higher education sector. Labeling all of these as for-profit institutions is problematic, however, given the growing market orientation of public and private nonprofit education in the United States and elsewhere. Where legal profit-making status exists, the institutions may not be considered part of the higher education system. In some countries, for-profit institutions cannot offer degrees; in others, they only offer degrees in partnerships with public-sector institutions. There are countries with ambiguous laws and regulations regarding for-profit education, or the rules that are in place may be unenforced, or simply ignored, in practice. In addition to local for-profit establishments, there are also several transnational providers, including U.S.-based Career Education, Kaplan, Laureate, and Whitney International; Australia-based IBT; South Africa-based Educor; and Singapore-based Raffles. However, most cross-border providers of education, even as they establish revenue-seeking operations abroad, are nonprofit or state-sponsored entities in their home countries. Continuing to complicate matters, the relationship may be reversed, with a company that is for-profit at home holding a controlling interest in a non-profit institution abroad.

All this means is that the global scope and impact of the for-profit sector is difficult to assess. Information is sketchy and incomplete. There are few comparative analyses available. Country-specific descriptions dominate the sparse literature, with idiosyncratic attempts to characterize the sector within local conditions. From this perspective, the U.S. case enjoys the most attention (Kinser & Levy, 2006) and, not incidentally, has the most comprehensive and reliable national data. Even so, there is widespread misunderstanding of for-profit higher education in the United States (Kinser, 2006b) that carries over to international assessments as well. Although the expansion of the for-profit sector in the United States over the last decade or so provides relevant comparisons to other countries, the higher education system in this country has characteristics and traditions that are exceptional in global summaries. U.S.-based corporations are major exporters of for-profit higher education around the world, yet most profit-oriented institutions are indigenous to their home country with personal connections to an individual owner (Kinser & Levy, 2006). Outside of the United States, large, publicly traded corporations are a new phenomenon, with companies such as AdvTech in South Africa, Eyas in Kuwait, and Kroton in Brazil becoming significant for-profit educational providers in their respective countries. Legitimacy issues plague even the well-established U.S. for-profits, even as the existence—and excellence—of the broader private sector remains unquestioned. In most other countries, however, skepticism regarding the for-profit form is subsumed within a larger debate over the legitimacy of an emerging or developing private higher education sector (cf. Slantcheva & Levy, 2007).

This chapter's titular purpose, therefore, of providing a global perspective on for-profit higher education is couched in understanding the U.S. case, but with the center of focus on the variety of models existing in other countries. Although this chapter, like much of the literature on for-profit higher education, is largely descriptive, a definitional frame for analyzing the sector is discussed first. Following that is an international tour of for-profit higher education, sketching its significance and regulatory status. The penultimate section expands the frame to discuss the for-profit approach to cross-border education and the role of profit-oriented entities in the educational trade. For-profit activity varies greatly from country to country, and the status of current research on the topic makes any summation tentative and preliminary. With that caveat, the chapter ends with several conclusions about for-profit higher education suggested by this global overview.

This chapter draws upon data gathered through the Program for Research on Private Higher Education (PROPHE), an international collaboration of scholars devoted to understanding the recent development of private higher education. Much of the information on non-U.S. cases comes from a survey conducted of the PROPHE network, and a selection of national laws and current news related to private higher education collected and summarized by PROPHE affiliates.[1] The private higher education literature that informs the larger PROPHE agenda also provides some context for how privateness and profit intermingle in countries where for-profit higher education has no formal status. Much of this literature was written or edited by PROPHE colleagues (e.g., Altbach & Levy, 2005).

The relationship of the U.S. case to the global for-profit phenomenon has been discussed in other writing (Kinser & Levy, 2006). Comparisons to the U.S. system will be tangential to the main agenda of identifying the for-profit focus internationally. As in the U.S., the for-profit sector globally is changing rapidly. The perspective offered here is a snapshot of current practice.

Definitional Complexities

As an initial point of departure, the definition of for-profit higher education should be understood as a complex and contentious subject. There are three main problems with a global definition of the sector: distinguishing for-profit from nonprofit, identifying "higher" education, and specifying legal impact of for-profit status.

Most basic is the lack of a globally relevant marker that divides the for-profit form from the nonprofit. In the United States, the tax code provides such a distinction. Importantly, the difference is gauged not in whether an institution enjoys excess revenue through its operations, but rather in what can be done with the money it generates: nonprofits must use their resources to continue the charitable purposes for which they were founded, whereas for-profits can sell shares in the company, pay dividends, invest in other businesses, liquidate all assets, or pursue completely unrelated activities. Countries without a history of private higher education often view all excess revenue as profit, even as they legally recognize the nonprofit form. Thus, a report by the International Institute for Educational Planning on private higher education in Bangladesh, Kenya, and several countries of the former Soviet Union (Varghese, 2002) refers to revenues minus expenses as profit, despite the fact that all of the institutions analyzed in detail are legally nonprofit entities in their countries. In Central and Eastern Europe, the majority of countries assume nonprofit forms for private higher education, even though by ownership and revenue expectations many resemble for-profit ventures (Slantcheva & Levy, 2007). Ukraine, however, upends this trend. All Ukrainian secular private higher education is for-profit, organized under the "law on business undertakings" and/or the "law on joint-stock companies"; religious schools are not considered educational institutions at all, and no accommodation is made for any nonprofit forms[2] (Stetar, Panych, & Tatsuko, 2007).

A second level of complexity to a global definition of for-profit higher education comes from variations in local context regarding what is considered "higher" education. International classifications of education identify the beginning of postsecondary education as Level 4, with tertiary starting at Level 5 (Organisation for Economic Cooperation and Development [OECD], 2004). In the U.S. case, this would roughly correspond to the divide between non–degree- and degree-granting schools, with most tabulators comfortable with categorizing the latter as higher education. In other countries, higher education is synonymous with universities, primarily OECD Level 6, sometimes including the upper reaches of Level 5. There are relatively few for-profit institutions of higher education by this standard, even in the United States. Including all Level 5 as higher education brings a more robust global tally of the for-profit sector, and the broader Level 4 standard quite probably includes most of the private tertiary institutions founded since the 1990s as part of the for-profit higher education universe.

Finally, even when one can surely identify the profit-making status of a set of institutions, it is not at all sure that they will be treated similarly in different countries. In most countries, for-profit institutions will pay taxes, though in Russia and Georgia, for example, so do the nonprofit institutions. By contrast, in Ukraine the law allows certain for-profits to avoid paying taxes. Subsidies to for-profit institutions are unusual, though a few countries follow the United States and allow state subsidies of student fees. New Zealand is an interesting case in that the 1989 authorizing legislation for private higher education makes no mention of profit status, treating all private institutions alike in their ability to participate in higher education (Abbott, 2005). This is opposite the general condition in many—perhaps most—other countries, where missing references to for-profit status are unplanned and result in legal ambiguity for the profit-oriented part of the private sector (Levy, 2006).

These definitional considerations are important in interpreting country reports on the for-profit sector. Poland, for example, has laws prohibiting for-profit higher education (i.e., universities), though for-profit vocational and nondegree postsecondary institutions are widespread. In the Nigerian case, one may eschew the legal for-profit/nonprofit divide and look to outsized fee levels to determine profitability, counting even religious institutions as for-profit because they are "part of the economic empires of their founders whether they are [legally] for-profit or not" (Obasi, 2006). In Chile, as in other countries with legally mandated nonprofit university status, the owners' return on investment can be achieved through indirect means, avoiding both formal dividends to shareholders and taxes to the government. Brazil and Peru, however, changed their laws to allow for-profit institutions in the 1990s, reasoning that if profit was being made, taxes should be paid (Levy, 2007).

The bottom line is that the for-profit status of a particular institution may be quite ambiguous. As a result, the scope of the sector globally is hard to pin down. If one takes a broad view of the phenomenon, it can seem that for-profit higher education dominates the private sector (Tilak, 2006). A strictly legal perspective suggests countries are increasingly recognizing the for-profit form, though formal status for profit-making institutions akin to the U.S. or New Zealand cases should still be considered against the norm. Focusing on university status reduces for-profit numbers still further, with Level 6 institutions—large, scholarly focused and post-baccalaureate— seemingly quite rare.

Several scholars have attacked the problem of distinguishing for-profit private higher education from its nonprofit cousin by focusing on the dynamics of private higher education in a particular country (Bernasconi, 2006; Praphamontripong, forthcoming; Suspitsin, 2007). All take Levy's (1986) analysis of demand-absorbing private higher education institutions as their launching point, and seek to understand the diversity of institutions that fall under this rubric. None of the countries in these analyses—Chile, Russia, and Thailand—has legally defined for-profit higher education, but the authors recognize that the profit motive is substantially involved in the development of some private higher education institutions. This profit-oriented subsector in each case is distinguished by reference to institutional ownership or affiliation. In the Chilean case, these are called "proprietary" institutions, implying control invested in a proprietor as opposed to affiliation with some external group. The similar designation of proprietary in Thailand is expanded to include company licensed institutions as well. The Russian example labels them Private Proper or Person Only. The key similarity here helps to focus attention away from their often ambiguous legal standing, or the institutional orientation to market forces (that sector spanning category would include many clearly public institutions as well as legal nonprofits), and looks to affiliation with a proprietor to find the central characteristic of for-profit higher education.[3]

With the variety of definitions identifying the for-profit sector globally, it is useful to distinguish those that are based on revenue generation and market sensitive activity from those that are based on ownership/affiliation and control. Excess revenue may be an indicator of institutional viability absent government subsidies, but surplus does not equal profit. Moreover, there is no guarantee that money can be made from privately financed education, regardless of the institution's founding mission. The market-focused behavior of demand-absorbing institutions need not be motivated by profit. Indeed, publicly financed educational initiatives to meet demand and serve economic development objectives are commonplace (the U.S. community college is a prime example). On the other hand, the ownership determines not only control over educational activities, but also the distribution and use of any profits generated from that activity. For-profit ownership includes, importantly, the ability to buy and sell shares of the enterprise, as well as the right to liquidate all holdings and exit the business entirely. For the purposes of global analysis, then, a definition of for-profit higher education based on proprietary ownership can be applied regardless of the local legal definition (or lack thereof) in a particular region.

To be clear, legal status and regulatory designations do continue to matter, and the following section will rely heavily on these formal labels in sketching the global scope of for-profit higher education. Market orientation, too, remains central to the activities of the for-profit providers. It is helpful, however, to define the for-profit sector based on proprietary affiliation, because it identifies the features of ownership and control necessary for a more meaningful comparative analysis even when there is no legal standing, or where market forces have significant influence.

For-Profit Higher Education Around the World

Around the world, public higher education dominates. Private higher education is expanding rapidly, although it currently accounts for less than a third of overall higher education enrollment (Levy, 2007). Majority private higher education enrollment is still rare, with only a handful of countries adopting models in which private sector provision takes the lead. The for-profit subset of private higher education is less extensive still. It is doubtful that any country yet has the majority of its students enrolled in legally for-profit institutions, although the Philippines may be close. Although typically a small subset by enrollment, for-profits may be rather large by institutional numbers. The U.S. case is instructive here, with for-profit institutions making up about 40% of all postsecondary institutions but just 8% of total enrollment. This follows patterns in other countries where private sector institutions, especially the new demand-absorbing ones, are small and numerous in comparison to the public sector. Another general trend also matching the U.S. case is the narrow academic focus of the for-profit sector. Most offer vocational programs at lower levels of education. Comprehensive universities, hard sciences, and the liberal arts are largely absent, as is most advanced professional education. For-profit institutions described in the following regional synopses are therefore more like the nondegree for-profits than like the expanding degree-granting institutions that have been responsible for the vast majority of the U.S. growth.

One additional point should be made explicit in discussing the global scope of for-profit higher education. It is an almost exclusively tuition-dependent exercise, and thus requires the state to allow fees to be charged for the provision of education. Explicit state subsidies are unusual, and few institutions make any substantial demands for government support. The U.S. case is unusual in that the for-profit sector relies heavily on government-sponsored student aid programs and has a powerful lobby to protect these subsidies (Kinser, 2007c; Pusser & Wolcott, 2006). More broadly, ersatz nonprofit institutions may receive tax breaks, and hidden subsidies can be significant in terms of real estate concessions, appropriating publicly developed curricula and moonlighting activities from public university employees (Kinser, 2005, 2006a; Tilak, 2006). Nevertheless, it should be emphasized that the for-profit sector exists as an essentially self-financed operation, directed toward those students and families with a disposable income sufficient to pay fees substantially higher than in the public sector.

In the discussion that follows, information on the for-profit presence in higher education is presented by region. Each regional description provides a sketch of the private role in education broadly and highlights the legal and de facto for-profit presence and regulatory models that currently exist in selected countries. Countries that are important providers or hosts for cross-border activity and foreign ownership are noted. Also noted are situations in which regional or country experiences match or contradict global trends. Because data on enrollments and institutional numbers are spotty, cross-regional quantitative comparisons are not attempted. Similarly, other information regarding regional or country-specific academic models, faculty standards, and the like are mostly anecdotal, if they exist at all. As a consequence, only the barest outline of the for-profit sector emerges. The full picture in any region, partially excepting North America, awaits a more comprehensive data collection process than currently exists.[4]

Africa

Only a few countries in Africa have a historical tradition of private higher education. Before the 1990s, the continent had only about thirty private institutions, with just a handful that could be considered commercially oriented. Expansion of the private sector occurred quickly after 1990, led by Kenya, Zaire, and South Africa. Other countries with now-large private enrollments include Benin, Ghana, Ivory Coast, Mozambique, Senegal, Tanzania, and Uganda (Levy, 2003). The new institutions have primarily been of the demand-absorbing, proprietary type. With the exception of South Africa, however, the for-profit form does not enjoy formal legal status in Africa. Nevertheless, clearly profit-oriented operation and owner motivations are widespread and accepted in practice, if not in law. Virtually all nonreligious institutions may be de facto for-profit (Teferra, 2006), especially at the nonuniversity levels (Levy, 2003); case studies of six countries in East Africa provide support for this assumption (Thaver, 2003). Liberia and Togo are unique in that profit-oriented institutions receive some government support. Other countries such as Tanzania and Uganda encourage tuition-dependent private higher education through dual-track tuition policies[5] (Teferra, 2006). With the exception of South Africa, the region is not a significant host or provider for cross-border initiatives.

The South African case is unusual for the explicit recognition of the for-profit form, and for the relatively few private institutions that choose to operate as nonprofits. Many for-profit institutions are listed on the Johannesburg stock market, including Educor's Midrand Graduate Institute, and public–private partnerships are widespread (Mabizela, 2005). This latter point is the case also in Ghana, where all private institutions are required to partner with a public-sector institution. Note that in South Africa, however, these partnerships are occurring between legally for-profit institutions and public universities. The owners of for-profit institutions include individual entrepreneurs, corporate business groups, and local small businesses. Since the emergence of the for-profit sector is relatively recent, the founders are often still in charge, and family run institutions are common (Levy, 2003). Even though South Africa is unusual with such a well-developed private for-profit system, its institutions largely match the global trend. Most operate in the vocational realm and, outside of narrowly defined fields, are hardly competitors to the traditional universities.

Asia

The private sector in many Asian countries has expanded rapidly. For-profit higher education is embedded within this expansion. Several countries have legally constituted for-profit institutions. Malaysia is a top example, with perhaps 90% of the private institutions operating for-profit (though accounting for a fraction of overall enrollment). As a capacity-building device, the government also encourages for-profit higher education through partnership agreements between Malaysian corporations and foreign providers. Singapore also looked to private for-profit education as a capacity-building initiative and to establish itself as a regional educational hub (Garrett, 2007). Singapore-based Raffles Education is a regional power, with locations in China, India, Malaysia, Mongolia, Thailand, Vietnam, Australia, and New Zealand.

In the Philippines, for-profit institutions, which have existed since World War II, represent a significant proportion of overall enrollment. The government responded to rising tuition rates first by mandating a cap on profits (at 12%) and then by banning the establishment of any new for-profit providers in the 1980s. China and India also have large for-profit sectors, although in both cases the legal status of these efforts face potential challenges. China allows "reasonable economic return" to be generated but considers this to be a government reward rather than profit. An ambiguously defined and government controlled definition of "reasonable" represents a compromise over a contentious concept in China (Yan & Levy, 2005). Indian courts have declared that education should not be conducted for private gain, and have ruled against the charging of certain fees. The impact this will have on domestic providers, however, is uncertain, though the foreign for-profit interest has been stymied. More recently, in 2004, Japan initiated an experiment in for-profit higher education, provisionally allowing the form to coexist with its dominant nonprofit higher education institutions.

Other Asian countries have profit-oriented institutions with uncertain legal status. Thailand has many private higher education institutions established and run by families, while Indonesia has a private sector run by foundations. In both cases the profit-generating capacity of these institutions suggests that some are not the purely charitable institutions the countries' laws assume. Like other developing economies in Central Asia, Mongolian higher education is transitioning away from sole government support, and a growing number of providers have stepped in to profit from the introduction of fees. Vietnam, too, has unfortunate experience with unscrupulous for-profit providers emerging within its "people-founded" private sector (Le & Ashwill, 2005). These cases make clear that corrupt organizations are ready to take advantage of a weak legal framework and weak oversight of the emerging private sector.[6]

Europe

The developed countries in Europe, outside of Portugal, have not experienced private higher education growth at the rate generally experienced in the rest of the world. A longstanding expectation that higher education be essentially free and supported by public funds has limited the potential of a fee-supported private sector, and thus the profit-oriented form. Still, many countries have for-profit institutions, though they are restricted in terms of university status and are not typically considered part of the higher education system. For-profit institutions owned by U.S.-based corporations are located in France, Germany, Ireland, the Netherlands, Spain, Switzerland, and the United Kingdom. Perhaps forecasting a changing European attitude toward fee-supported higher education, Germany and the U.K. have moved to allow for-profit degree-granting institutions.

The private surge has been important in Eastern and Central Europe, as post-communist countries adopted market reforms and used the private sector to build capacity (Slantcheva & Levy, 2007). Though only occasionally acknowledged, the for-profit demand-absorbing form is much in evidence in the private expansion. The Ukraine case is unique in that all private higher education is legally for-profit, which is a result of extreme skepticism at the idea that nonprofit institutions could be both incorruptible and altruistic organizations. Poland is more like its Western European neighbors in prohibiting for-profit degree-granting institutions but allowing nonuniversity and professional courses to be offered in the for-profit sector. In other countries, for-profit higher education was initially accepted, and then prohibited. Romania is a good example here. The country banned for-profits in 1995, but many still maintain the preregulatory profit orientation. Turkey also made a similar decision to eliminate a growing for-profit sector, albeit in the 1970s, but recent developments have seen publicly traded Laureate Education add Istanbul Bilgi University to its international network. Laureate also owns an institution in Cyprus. The Russian case typifies the quick profit-oriented growth of the private sector, followed by regulatory changes that ostensibly require nonprofit status. Typical also is uneven enforcement. As in many countries, what laws and regulations say on the books does not always translate to behavior on the ground. Along with Georgia, Russian nonprofits pay taxes, further suggesting the Eastern European ambivalence toward these institutions.

Latin America

With its history of religious private higher education and new private expansion, Latin America represents an important case for investigating the role of for-profit provision within the private sector. The archetype demand-absorbing private form was identified here (Levy, 1986), thus providing the ancestor to the current focus on defining and classifying for-profit higher education in legally ambiguous systems. The region also boasts two countries, Brazil and Peru, with recognized for-profit higher education. As previously mentioned, for-profit higher education was legalized in these countries to bring institutions' de jure status in line with their de facto operation. In other countries, such as Mexico and Uruguay, for-profit higher education is explicitly prohibited, and in Chile only non-university for-profit provision is allowed. Mexico, however, is an example similar to that in other regions, where the nonprofit form is required even as institutions are able to operate as profit-oriented organizations. Sometimes this activity is rather obvious, as the many Mexican technical campuses suggest.

Foreign-owned institutions play a large role in the region. Laureate and Whitney International operate in several countries, with the former clearly the more formidable actor. Apollo, despite several false starts, is only just beginning to get established in the region, with a University of Phoenix campus in a Mexican border town. Again, Mexico represents an interesting phenomenon seen in the region whereby foreign for-profit ownership is allowed even when domestic laws prohibit the for-profit form. This seems to be the case in Argentina, Chile, Columbia, Costa Rica, Ecuador, and Panama, where Laureate and Whitney have ownership stakes in private higher education institutions. The status of the foreign-owned institutions in these countries also points to ambiguities in what is considered "higher" education and therefore profit-prohibited.

Middle East

Private higher education in much of the Middle East is explicitly connected to modernization, and the model adopted is thoroughly American. The Gulf states in particular have devoted substantial resources to develop new higher education institutions. Because of religious and cultural demands that limit the ability of women to travel abroad for education, the educational focus has been oriented toward females, and the private sector has accommodated. This well represents the demand-absorbing role identified with the recent global surge in private higher education (Levy, 2006) and also suggests the access role that for-profit institutions serve—as is often argued in the U.S. case (Kinser, 2006a).

For-profit education is implicitly or explicitly accepted in several countries in the region. Jordan has nonprofit and for-profit higher education, and profit-oriented institutions are the dominant providers for noncitizen guest workers in Saudi Arabia and Kuwait. These latter countries encourage foreign providers, but Qatar and United Arab Emirates (UAB) are the major importers of education in the region. Though the providing institutions are mostly elite private and public institutions, in country they are considered for-profit enterprises. Ensuring sufficient revenue to make the operation viable is part of the commitment made by Qatar and UAB as they have established education cities to host foreign education providers. Other providers are owned by for-profit corporations and venture capital organizations seeking investments in the wealthy region (Spindle, 2007). Some for-profit institutions have established branch campuses, notably Career Education's American Intercontinental University. The U.S. occupation of Iraq apparently opened the door for a new private university that seems to parallel the for-profit model even though it is legally nonprofit (Krieger, 2007). The American University of Iraq is led by an Iraqi minister, an example of government-connected founding well traveled by certain profit-oriented institutions established in Russia (Suspitsin, 2007).

For-Profit and Cross-Border Higher Education

Cross-border higher education—also labeled transnational, borderless, or offshore education—refers to the movement of people, programs, providers, and projects across national boundaries (Green, Eckel, Calderon, & Luu, 2007). This includes not only the traditional exchange programs and study abroad programs, but also international branch campuses, distance delivery of academic programs, and foreign investment in educational institutions. For-profit higher education is engaged across the spectrum of cross-border activity, but is especially connected to providing physical or virtual access to programs from an exporting country in a host country. It should be noted, however, that even in this capacity, for-profit entities play a minor role compared to state-funded and private nonprofit higher education institutions (Verbik & Merkley, 2006). Nevertheless, virtually all cross-border higher education is (or is intended to be) self-supporting, based on revenue generated by local student tuition and fees (McBurnie & Ziguras, 2007). From the perspective of the host country, it most often looks like for-profit higher education regardless of the exporting organization's legal status (Daniel, Kanwar, & Uvalic-Trumbic, 2006).

In addition to the complexities and ambiguities associated with indigenous for-profit higher education, cross-border providers must also navigate the global trade barriers most countries have in place. In education, attempts to remove barriers are often rather contentious, fueled by fears of privatization and loss of local control of schooling. Quality assurance is a significant challenge as well, given the lack of a global framework for recognizing legitimate higher education institutions and the variety of state-sponsored and nongovernmental accreditation models in existence (Larson & Momii, 2004; Vincent-Lancrin, 2007). The debate over the inclusion of education in the General Agreement on Trade in Services (GATS) is emblematic of these contentious and challenging issues (Lane, Brown, & Pearcey, 2004). For-profit higher education involvement in global trade issues is important not because of the extent of current operations, but because of assumptions that these agreements will open up markets to future activities. These assumptions are aggravated by the resistance in many parts of the world to treating education as a commodity (McBurnie & Ziguras, 2007). Indeed, ongoing conversations between the American Council on Education and the U.S. Trade Representative to the GATS talks seems to suggest that the motivating factor for U.S. efforts to liberalize trade in education comes from the for-profit sector, and not the broader higher education community (American Council on Education, 2007).

There is a difference, though, between formalizing trade policy regarding cross-border education—which via GATS is a hard slog—and actually engaging in exporting educational services through individualized arrangements with importing countries. This latter approach is the current trend (Garrett & Verbik, 2004; Verbik & Merkley, 2006). Again, relatively few for-profit entities are involved. Out of eighty-two institutions with transnational branch campuses, just six are sponsored by for-profit providers (Verbik & Merkley, 2006). But the interest that the for-profit sector has in global expansion is clear. Worldwide participation rates in higher education are relatively low. In general, this is not because of weak demand, but rather because of a lack of sufficient space to meet the demand. Governments are unwilling or unable to fund public institutions to increase capacity, leading to a rise in privately financed postsecondary options (Levy, 2006). At the same time, increased demand by and competition for students and their tuition dollars push owners to look for new markets (Kinser, 2007a). They are finding markets not just in the developed countries of Europe and Asia, but now also in the large populations of the developing world (Daniel, Kanwar, & Uvalic-Trumbic, 2006). There are at least six different ways in which for-profit higher education participates in cross-border activities.[7]

Foreign Ownership

Foreign ownership of local institutions likely has engaged the strongest involvement of for-profit entities. The dominant example here is Laureate Education. Beginning with the acquisition of Universidad Europea de Madrid in 1999, Laureate has steadily built an international network of twenty-three postsecondary institutions with locations in Latin America, Europe, and China.[8] The Laureate strategy identifies well-established institutions with good local reputations and then invests in their continued operations. It seeks to develop synergies across institutions rather than duplicating operational activities. In other words, Laureate's goal is to build enrollment at each institution as an operationally independent entity, concentrating on increasing efficiency through the economies of scale that network membership brings. This strategy allows Laureate to develop financially profitable relationships with institutions in the network that are not themselves for-profit entities in their home countries (e.g., Universidad Andrés Bello in Chile). A similar strategy is being pursued by several other U.S.-based owners, including Whitney International University System and Kaplan Higher Education. Changes in the regulatory environment in host countries may encourage or discourage this activity. For example, Laureate pulled out of plans to invest in India in the face of uncertainty regarding the ability for higher education institutions in that country to continue operating for profit.

Branch Campuses

A second model involves establishing branch campuses, exemplified by Raffles Education Corporation. The company has expanded its Raffles Design Institute brand into eight countries throughout Asia and added the multinational Hartford Institute in 2004. Unlike Laureate, Raffles develops original programs for distribution via its network. Profit comes through economies of scale associated with central control over the curriculum, and the regional familiarity of the Raffles (and Hartford) brand creates a common frame that reduces startup costs for new institutions and programs. This strategy is followed by other owners, such as Educor (in Africa) and the U.S.-based Apollo Group. It seems, though, that it is difficult to export name-brand institutions outside of the home country and its near neighbors. Establishing branch campuses is resource-intensive, and with regulatory issues in flux in many countries, the risks are high (Verbik & Merkley, 2006). The Apollo Group, for example, has been attempting to expand its University of Phoenix brand internationally since at least 2000, with limited success. A branch campus in Juarez (sister city to El Paso, Texas) and a couple of locations in Canada, represent the company's major accomplishments to date despite all the talk of impending partnerships and acquisitions in India, China, and South America.[9]

Internationalization

A third form of cross-border provision comes from institutions that have developed an international identity, with branch campuses serving as opportunities for students to study abroad more than they cater to host country populations. This form has a longstanding presence in traditional private nonprofit and public higher education. The for-profit institutions that follow this model typically look to take advantage of a market niche—fashion design in London for American Intercontinental University, or transferable American-style degrees offered in Europe for Schiller International University—and promote their offerings as cross-cultural experiences. These for-profit schools can develop profitable relationships with public and private nonprofit institutions to serve as the host campus for their study abroad programs. Branch campuses may evolve into their own independent entities—the U.S. International University in Kenya for example—after the parent institution decides to exit.[10] In this case, they become local providers, though in-country the former relationship with the foreign country could still serve as a market distinction.

Curriculum Supply

A fourth model involves the sale of curricular materials to a partner institution in the host country. This is often portrayed as a capacity-building activity, whereby the local institution is able to quickly deliver advanced programs where there is little indigenous expertise. The best programs of this sort also involve on-site trainers and advisors to help adapt curricula to local conditions. They have, however, also been tagged as diploma mill operators that simply trick students into thinking they are getting an authorized foreign degree that has neither the quality or substance of the original. Vietnam's experience in this is cautionary.

Partnerships

Fifth is a model that involves formal partnership arrangements. In this system, the host country requires or encourages the exporting institution to provide the education in conjunction with a local entity. China is an important host of this model, as is South Africa. The local source does not even have to be an educational institution, as the case in Malaysia, where real estate companies have linked with foreign education providers to establish campuses connected to new residential developments. The partnership model is different in that it often involves a nonprofit or public institution as the foreign source, with a private for-profit partner in country. Partnerships are generally promoted in the host country as a capacity-building policy, and typically are government-controlled in order to ensure compatibility with national goals (Vincent-Lancrin, 2004).

Distance Delivery

The final model for for-profit cross-border education is distance delivery. This is more difficult to document, because it does not involve physical presence in the receiving country. It is likely, though, that most major distance education institutions have active enrollments in foreign countries whether or not they market to the nondomestic audience. Some for-profit institutions promote their distance models and recruit internationally. The University of Phoenix online division, for example, has a special Web site directed toward international students. Many institutions accredited by the Distance Education and Training Council in the U.S. parlay their American accreditation—attractive in many countries—to advertise their programs internationally. These are, of course, reputable institutions, but the sketchy reputation of for-profit distance education internationally should not be ignored. Not only do diploma mill institutions attempt to take advantage of students through worthless distance offerings, "accreditation mills" also provide worthless authorization to these programs, making regulation of the industry all the more difficult (Ezell, 2007).

Conclusion

This global portrait of for-profit higher education necessarily involves partial descriptions and convenient sampling. A coherent database of information does not exist. There has been limited scholarly attention to the phenomenon, with country or regionally specific accounts forming the bulk of the literature. Sources on the topic are marked by inconsistent definitions and conflicting perspectives. Generalizations are hazardous in this environment. Nevertheless, this chapter will hazard six broad conclusions that can be drawn from the preceding discussion.

Defining the For-Profit Form

First, local definitions of for-profit higher education are often misleading, especially if viewed through a U.S. perspective that makes clear legal distinctions in profit-making status. Not only do for-profit and nonprofit sectors blur in global comparisons, but public-sector institutions have also been encouraged to accept fee-supported financing by a dominating neoliberal privatization agenda. In some countries, definitional ambiguity is abetted by the lack of an established nonprofit sector, in education or elsewhere, such that privately financed operations have few eleemosynary models to follow. The profit-oriented form therefore emerges out of an entrepreneurial spirit, driven by growing demand and restricted state support. At the same time, it is embedded within an environment that presumes the public purpose of education, and in which the nonprofit form may be culturally or legally preferred. It should not be surprising that discussions of private higher education will variously ignore the for-profit form or overestimate its significance.

The assumptions that are embedded in local definitions are not always stated but almost always involve questions of revenue, activity, and control. Does the institution charge fees and generate excess revenue? Does it serve a demand-absorbing[11] function with a vocationally focused curriculum? Is there a controlling owner who manages the institution as personal property? Because affirmative answers to the first two questions cause inevitable confusion with entrepreneurial nonprofit and public institutions, a globally relevant definition of for-profit higher education should center on the ownership model of the institution rather than on institutional activities or revenue surplus.

Cross-Border as For-Profit

Second, cross-border education is becoming increasingly common on the global stage, and a growing number of explicitly for-profit providers are engaged in educational trade. Still, most cross-border activity involves a private nonprofit or public higher education institution as the exporting entity. When for-profit providers are involved, it may be in partnership with legally nonprofit institutions in the host country. Conversely, nonprofit providers may partner with for-profit entities, or may consider themselves to be for-profit organizations when they deliver fee-based educational services.

The complicated patterns that emerge in cross-border higher education make it a significant exception to an ownership-based definition of the for-profit sector. The financial and governance arrangements between the parent entities and their profit-oriented subsidiaries must become part of the definitional calculus. Where the initiative is intended to develop new revenue streams or serves primarily to subsidize other core functions, it is appropriate to consider the profit motive primary. The closing of financially unviable cross-border initiatives in South Africa, Malaysia, and Singapore, for example, demonstrates the reluctance of providers to sustain a cross-border relationship absent a sufficient return on investment. Therefore, cross-border education should in most cases be considered a for-profit activity, irrespective of the ownership status of the providing entity in its home country.

For-Profit "Higher" Education

A third conclusion addresses the issue of whether for-profit education should be considered "higher" education. On the one hand, it is appropriate to question the educational status of for-profit institutions, particularly when they adopt the title and symbolic form of traditional universities without the academic infrastructure or standards to back it up (Altbach, 2001). On the other hand, the broader postsecondary universe has great significance to the educational development of most countries. The economic importance of education creates a demand for tertiary instruction, and the demand-absorbing institutions that result are largely for-profit in character.

To the extent to which one emphasizes the higher levels of educational activity, the role of the for-profit sector diminishes. For-profit postsecondary education, however, is often widespread in countries that prohibit for-profit higher education in their universities. Ignoring this may lead to a false sense of the irrelevance of the profit-oriented form to educational activity. A shift in for-profit sector focus can come quickly—witness the rapid emergence of degree-granting for-profit higher education in the United States—and cause traumatic change in an unaware higher education establishment and state policy apparatus. It is better to be informed. The inclusion of lower postsecondary levels in discussions of for-profit higher education is warranted.

Assumptions of For-Profit Status

Fourth, the legal status of for-profit higher education is often contentious. Previously noted definitional assumptions introduce variability in how institutions are labeled, but where legal for-profit status is available, the regulatory framework makes its own assumptions about these institutions and how they should be treated. These assumptions can be categorized in two forms. For-profit status may be considered a distinct form, with institutions assumed to be businesses quite separate from true educational organizations (which remain public or nonprofit in character). Alternatively, for-profits may essentially be seen as a subset of the private sector, with policy assuming they are educational organizations first, profit-making entities second.

In the case of for-profit higher education as a distinct form, profit through fees/tuition is interpreted as an economic rather than an educational activity. This perspective sees revenue generation as the near exclusive purpose of a for-profit institution, with education serving as the product of the firm. From the alternate perspective of for-profit higher education as a private-sector institution, profit from fees/tuition is used for educational as well as economic ends. This distinction emphasizes that for-profit status is distinguished not by generating excess revenue, but by the ends to which that excess revenue can be put. It is interesting to note that the regulatory efforts across countries range from a laissez-faire attitude to one of restrictive supervision, with examples to be found under each assumption.

For-Profit Distribution

A fifth conclusion suggests the breadth of distribution of the for-profit form. Regionally, Asian countries seem to be most engaged in for-profit higher education, but the phenomenon is truly global. Every region has strong examples of for-profit presence. Conversely, every region has examples of significant prohibitions of the for-profit form. The for-profit cross-border phenomenon has also made a global impact, although the delivery is one-way. Providers in developed countries establish profit-oriented offshore sites in developing countries, frequently in capacity-building partnerships with local institutions or organizations in the host country. For-profit entities have established a global footprint through the direct foreign ownership of higher education institutions, even in countries where the for-profit form is not recognized.

Increasingly—and following the trend of private higher education growth (Levy, 2006)—countries are recognizing the existence of for-profit higher education within their boundaries. Regulating excess revenue earned by new private providers, for example, is a de facto recognition of the profit-making form, leading to de jure distinctions among institutions. Globally, the for-profit sector tends to be most apparent in those countries that have large private higher education sectors (in terms of numbers of institutions) serving a largely demand-absorbing function. Still, much remains under the radar. The contentious status of profit in education can make it culturally invisible, while local definitional ambiguity can make it easy to deny. Countries where for-profits are more evident may simply be those where policymakers and institutional leaders have paid more attention.

Typical For-Profit Institution

Finally, the bulk of for-profit higher education is concentrated in small institutions serving the local community with lower-level credentials. This is probably the most universal conclusion one can draw from examining for-profit higher education worldwide. And in this, the U.S. case is typical, with its preponderance of non–degree-granting for-profit schools. In the United States, though, the sector has expanded over the last decade or so by developing its degree-granting function, with large, well-funded multicampus institutions establishing brand name recognition across the country. This is not seen in most other countries. It is important to recognize, however, that U.S. for-profits have undergone enormous transition in a relatively short period of time. Other countries with better-developed institutions and regulatory systems may be on the cusp of a similar transformation.

Even though foreign ownership is a growing phenomenon, there are few multinational for-profit institutions. That is, it is rare for a for-profit institution to establish a branch campus in another country outside of its immediate neighborhood. The potential of this sort of expansion, however, is suggested by the success of multistate institutions in the United States. Nevertheless, it is currently easier for capital to cross borders through acquisitions than through the export of name-brand programs.

In sum, this chapter highlights the status of for-profit higher education outside the United States. The profit-oriented form is significant globally, even though it has an ambiguous existence in many places and questionable legitimacy almost everywhere. The broader trend toward privatization and the impact of globalization opens space for considering the profit potential of education, whether legally sanctioned or not. Even so, the potential of for-profit higher education remains greater than its reality. The public sector still dominates; the state continues to serve as the controlling authority in education. The significance of for-profit higher education, therefore, comes from its emblematic status as an alternative educational model, its evolving impact on traditional higher education institutions, and the various state policy responses to an emerging private sector.

References

Abbott, M. (2005). *Private higher education penetration into a mature education market: The New Zealand experience* (Working Paper #6). Albany, NY: Program for Research on Private Higher Education, University at Albany, SUNY.

Altbach, P. G. (2001). The rise of the pseudouniversity. *International Higher Education, 25*(Fall), 2–3.

Altbach, P. G., & Levy, D. C. (Eds.). (2005). *Private higher education: A global revolution.* Rotterdam: Sense Publishers.

American Council on Education. (2007). *U.S. update on the GATS negotiations and issues for higher education: March 2007.* Washington, DC: American Council on Education.

Bernasconi, A. (2006). Does the affiliation of universities to external organizations foster diversity in private higher education? Chile in comparative perspective. *Higher Education, 52*, 303–342.

Daniel, J., Kanwar, A., & Uvalic-Trumbic, S. (2006). A tectonic shift in global higher education. *Change, 38*(4), 16–23.

Ezell, A. (2007). *Accreditation mills.* Washington, DC: American Association of Collegiate Registrars and Admissions Officers.

Ezell, A., & Bear, J. (2005). *Degree mills: The billion-dollar industry that has sold over a million fake diplomas.* Amherst, NY: Prometheus Books.

Garrett, R. (2007, February 1). *For-profit higher education internationally: Trends and issues.* Paper presented at the Council for Higher Education Accreditation International Meeting, Washington, DC.

Garrett, R., & Verbik, L. (2004). Transnational higher education: Major markets and emerging trends. In S. Bjarnason (Ed.), *Mapping borderless higher education: Policy, markets and competition: Selected reports from the Observatory on Borderless Higher Education* (pp. 319–374). London: The Observatory on Borderless Higher Education.

Green, M. F., Eckel, P. D., Calderon, L., & Luu, D. T. (2007). *Venturing abroad: Delivering U.S. degrees through overseas branch campuses and programs.* Washington, DC: American Council on Education.

Kinser, K. (2005). Faculty at private for-profit universities: The University of Phoenix as a new model? In P. G. Altbach & D. C. Levy (Eds.), *Private higher education: A global revolution* (pp. 273–276). Rotterdam: Sense Publishers.

Kinser, K. (2006a). *From Main Street to Wall Street: The transformation of for-profit higher education.* ASHE Higher Education Report Series (Vol. 31:5). San Francisco: Jossey-Bass.

Kinser, K. (2006b). What Phoenix doesn't teach us about for-profit higher education. *Change, 38*(4), 24–29.

Kinser, K. (2007a). Dimensions of corporate ownership of for-profit higher education. *Review of Higher Education, 30*(3), 217–245.

Kinser, K. (2007b, March 30). For-profit institutions need to be classified, too. *Chronicle of Higher Education,* pp. B9–B10.

Kinser, K. (2007c). Sources of legitimacy in U.S. for-profit higher education. In S. Slantcheva & D. C. Levy (Eds.), *Private higher education in post-communist Europe: In search of legitimacy* (pp. 257–276). New York: Palgrave MacMillan.

Kinser, K., & Levy, D. C. (2006). For-profit higher education: U.S. tendencies, international echoes. In J. Forest & P. Altbach (Eds.), *The international handbook of higher education* (pp. 107–119). Dordrecht, the Netherlands and London, UK: Springer Publishers.

Krieger, Z. (2007, August 17). Born in Iraq: An American University. *Chronicle of Higher Education,* p. A35.

Lane, J. E., Brown, M. C., & Pearcey, M. A. (2004). Transnational campuses: Obstacles and opportunities for institutional research in the global education market. In J. E. Lane & M. C. Brown (Eds.), *Examining unique campus settings: Insights for research and assessment* (New Directions for Institutional Research, vol. 124, pp. 49–62). San Francisco: Jossey-Bass.

Larson, K., & Momii, K. (Eds.). (2004). *Quality and recognition in higher education: The cross-border challenge.* Paris: Organisation for Economic Cooperation and Development.

Le, N. M., & Ashwill, M. A. (2005). Nonpublic private higher education in Vietnam. In P. G. Altbach & D. C. Levy (Eds.), *Private higher education: A global revolution* (pp. 159–162). Rotterdam: Sense Publishers.

Levy, D. C. (1986). *Higher education and the state in Latin America: Private challenges to public dominance.* Chicago: University of Chicago Press.

Levy, D. C. (2003). *Profits and practicality: How South Africa epitomizes the global search and commercial private higher education* (Working Paper #2). Albany, NY:

Program for Research on Private Higher Education, University at Albany, SUNY.

Levy, D. C. (2006). The unanticipated explosion: Private higher education's global surge. *Comparative Education Review, 50*(2), 217–240.

Levy, D. C. (2007, January 17). *Private-public interfaces in higher education development: Two sectors in sync?* Paper presented at the Conference on Higher Education and Development: The 2007 World Bank Regional Seminar on Development Economics, Beijing.

Mabizela, M. (2005). *The business of higher education: A study of public-private partnerships in the provision of higher education in South Africa.* Monograph. Research Programme on Human Resources Development, Human Sciences Research Council, Cape Town, South Africa.

Maio, P. (2007, April 24). Apollo group hires key executive to help M&A expansion internationally, analysts say. *Financial Times.*

McBurnie, G., & Ziguras, C. (2007). *Transnational education: Issues and trends in offshore higher education.* New York: Routledge.

Obasi, I. N. (2006). *The sustainability question of private universities in Nigeria: Ownership, fees and the market.* Presentation made at the State University of New York at Albany, New York, Program for Research on Private Higher Education, Albany, New York.

Organisation for Economic Cooperation and Development. (2004). *OECD handbook for internationally comparative education statistics: Concepts, standards, definitions and classifications.* Paris: Author.

Praphamontripong, P. (forthcoming). *Institutional differentiation in Thai private higher education: Exploring private growth in international context* (Working Paper Series). Albany, NY: Program for Research on Private Higher Education, University at Albany, SUNY.

Pusser, B., & Wolcott, D. A. (2006). A crowded lobby: Nonprofit and for-profit universities in the emerging politics of higher education. In D. Breneman, B. Pusser & S. Turner (Eds.), *Earnings from learning: The rise of for-profit universities* (pp. 167–194). Albany, NY: State University of New York Press.

Slantcheva, S., & Levy, D. C. (Eds.). (2007). *Private higher education in post-communist Europe: In search of legitimacy.* New York: Palgrave MacMillan.

Spindle, B. (2007, July 19). Boom in investment powers mideast growth. *Wall Street Journal.*

Stetar, J., & Panych, O. (2007). Ukraine. In P. J. Wells, J. Sadlak, & L. Vl_sceanu (Eds.), *The rising role and relevance of private higher education in Europe* (pp. 519–584). Bucharest: UNESCO, CEPES.

Stetar, J., Panych, O., & Tatusko, A. (2007). State power in legitimating and regulating private higher education: The case of Ukraine. In S. Slantcheva &

D. C. Levy (Eds.), *Private higher education in post-communist Europe: In search of legitimacy* (pp. 239–256). New York: Palgrave MacMillan.

Suspitsin, D. (2007). Between the state and the market: Sources of sponsorship and legitimacy in Russian nonstate higher education. In S. Slantcheva & D. C. Levy (Eds.), *Private higher education in post-communist Europe: In search of legitimacy* (pp. 157–178). New York: Palgrave MacMillan.

Teferra, D. (2006). Financing higher education in Sub-Saharan Africa. In J. Tres & F. López-Segrera (Eds.), *Higher education in the world 2006: The financing of universities* (pp. 153–164). New York: Palgrave MacMillan.

Thaver, B. (2003). Private higher education in Africa: Six country case studies. In P. G. Altbach & D. Teferra (Eds.), *Africa higher education: An international reference handbook* (pp. 53–60). Bloomington: Indiana University Press.

Tilak, J. B. G. (2006). Private higher education: Philanthropy to profits. In J. Tres & F. López-Segrera (Eds.), *Higher education in the world 2006: The financing of universities* (pp. 113–121). New York: Palgrave MacMillan.

Varghese, N. V. (Ed.). (2002). *Private higher education.* Paris: International Institute for Educational Planning.

Verbik, L., & Merkley, C. (2006). *The international branch campus: Models and trends.* London: Observatory on Borderless Higher Education.

Vincent-Lancrin, S. (2004). *Internationalisation and trade in higher education: Opportunities and challenges.* Paris: Organisation for Economic Cooperation and Development.

Vincent-Lancrin, S. (Ed.). (2007). *Cross-border tertiary education: A way towards capacity development.* Paris: Organisation For Economic Cooperation and Development.

Yan, F., & Levy, D. C. (2005). China's new private higher education law. In P. G. Altbach & D. C. Levy (Eds.), *Private higher education: A global revolution* (pp. 113–116). Rotterdam: Sense Publishers.

Endnotes

[1] Available at http://www.albany.edu/dept/eaps/prophe.

[2] The law technically allows nonprofit higher education (Stetar & Panych, 2007), but the availability of this status is either ignored or does not seem to apply to any Ukrainian institutions.

[3] The U.S. case also shows how affiliation is important to classification, not only representing a dividing line between for-profit and nonprofit, but also serving to distinguish the many types of for-profit institutions based on controlling ownership (Kinser, 2007b).

⁴ Data drawn from the PROPHE network is clearly not comprehensive, with limitations in country coverage and collaborators' knowledge of the for-profit form as a distinct subset of private higher education, the latter being the target of PROPHE work.

⁵ The government supports a certain proportion of students while encouraging private institutions to enroll the remaining fee-paying students.

⁶ This is the case in developed countries, too. In the United States, a scandalous degree mill industry is the result of several states' lax oversight of private higher education (Ezell & Bear, 2005).

⁷ A different, but overlapping, typology for cross-border tertiary education from the OECD emphasizes program mobility rather than ownership of the program (Vincent-Lancrin, 2007).

⁸ The company also owns the online Walden University as its only U.S.-based postsecondary institution.

⁹ A Phoenix location in the Netherlands has apparently operated at a loss since its inception. Apollo has recently hired a new executive to head up its sputtering international agenda (Maio, 2007).

¹⁰ The former parent of USIU in Kenya was a nonprofit university, and the institution maintains that status through its U.S. corporate organization. But because it earns surplus revenue, it is described as a for-profit institution within Kenya's system (Varghese, 2004).

¹¹ Unmet demand implies a new market for education where fees can be charged, as opposed to a system constrained by public (and philanthropic) financing without opportunities for fee-driven institutions.

8

THE PUBLIC GOOD IN
A CHANGING ECONOMY

William G. Tierney

E ducation has long been seen as a public good in the United States. Such a simple observation, however, has always had a degree of complexity with regard to *content, form,* and *definition.* The *content* of what the public has meant by "education" has been a series of long-standing battles that some suggest go to the heart of what we mean by democracy. Is the content of the curriculum geared for training or involved with larger issues such as citizenship development? Public schools and private schools, and whether taxpayers should fund private schools, have been a core concern over the *form* of education for over a century. For example, Catholic parents desirous of having their children receive a Catholic education have advocated for subsidies of their schools; others have argued that public monies for education should only go to nondenominational schooling. Obviously, with the rise of charter schools, vouchers, homeschooling, and the like, the debate over the form of education has only increased. And whether education is a public good, or how much of a public good it is as opposed to a private benefit is a matter of *definition* that continues to be debated in state legislatures and Congress.

The discussion over higher education as a public good has been similar to, yet different from, that of K–12 education. Although the citizenry has long argued over what content should be taught in colleges and universities, the discussions are more muted than they are in elementary and secondary education. The public has been more willing to cede curricular authority to the faculty than to schoolteachers. Thus, issues such as evolution are pitched content-related battles in K–12, but not in higher education. The larger issue of content elides with that of form. What is the purpose of a postsecondary education, and how do the various postsecondary forms support or detract from such purposes? Those who suggest that a postsecondary education is an advanced form of training will point to community colleges as the provider of choice. Those who argue that a postsecondary education should be devoted to the life of the mind, learning for learning's sake, training to participate in a democracy, and the like often look askance at educational forms such as community colleges and admire what is offered at institutions such as Harvard or Stanford or liberal arts colleges such as Oberlin and Swarthmore.

The discussion over the public good also is a bit more complex. There is general agreement today that all youth need education through high school, but how much of a postsecondary education a person needs is a matter for debate. The consequence is that some will argue that postsecondary education is not a public good, whereas others will claim that a college education is a public good today as a consequence of the advanced training needs of the citizenry due to globalization. Still others will say that education—as defined by teaching students—is only part of the function of a postsecondary institution and the additional tasks—research, argumentation, academic freedom—are central to the public good.

For-profit higher education, as a relatively new significant entrant to the postsecondary marketplace, has added to the complexity of the argument over postsecondary education as a public good. Some will argue that the content of for-profit higher education is problematic for many reasons—quality being the most prominent concern. The actual "form" of for-profit higher education, of course, is distinctly different from traditional higher education. Although for-profits have been in existence for over a century, their growth as companies and corporations has forced the higher education community to ask whether form trumps content. Does it matter that a group that makes money but provides a similar service to a nonprofit partake of public monies? Such a question, of course, not only pertains to the form an educational service takes but also relates to the nature of how a society defines "public good." These questions and concerns, although related to previous discussions about K–12 and postsecondary education, are also different because the providers are for-profit. Catholic schools were a different form with a different content from their public school counterparts, but they were nonprofit. Community colleges have a different content from their liberal arts confreres, but they are all public (or private nonprofit).

For-profit colleges and universities, then, enable us to consider old questions in new ways. In what follows, I first outline the postsecondary world today by discussing the various forms that exist, and consider where for-profits fit into that world. I then turn to a discussion of the changing nature of the public good and how for-profit higher education fits into the picture. This is an *essai* in the root nature of the word—a trial of some ideas. A topic such as the public good is different from arguments over quality, learning outcomes, teaching productivity, and the like insofar as topics such as those presumably have empirical strength in that they can be measured. One might argue with one or another measurement, but such a discussion is distinctly different from that over the public good which, as I shall elaborate, is essentially a discussion over the kind of society a citizenry wishes to have.

Higher Education as a Growth Industry

Those who work in shrinking or stable markets frequently look askance at new providers. Upstart airlines, for example, often have had hurdles placed in front of them by more traditional competitors afraid that a new entrant may take away some of their market share. A related concern is that the quality of the new entrant will be so low that it will not only impact its own organization but also affect consumer confidence in the larger industry. At the same time, the United States, as a capitalist nation, always has tried to balance the desire to promote healthy competition with the need to have regulatory oversight to ensure that the consumer is protected and businesses actually are competing fairly. To be sure, traditional businesses frequently have exerted pressure upon legislatures and in the marketplace so that the new companies have had a harder time competing. Nevertheless, the United States has tried, in theory, to follow the dictum of the market that competition aids the overall economy by providing the consumer with choices.

The reaction by traditional providers in the higher education market (nonprofit colleges and universities) has not been unlike their counterparts in other industries to the entrance of the new entrants (for-profit colleges and universities), with one exception. Those in traditional postsecondary institutions either have looked askance at for-profits and worried about the quality of the product, or they have been troubled that for-profits might be stealing some of their market share. The result is that traditional colleges and universities (TCUs) have sought regulatory oversight and used the marketplace to see if they might constrain for-profits. The one significant difference with this market, however, is that higher education is a growth industry that many feel is incapable of ramping up to meet the insatiable need for more postsecondary education in the United States and throughout the world. Why, then, should TCUs worry about a minor player in a growing industry?

In 2006, the United States had 6,700 postsecondary institutions, 2,700 of which were four-year, 2,220 of which were two-year, and the remainder of which were less than two-year. The increase in overall institutions from the previous year was about 1.5 percent, and the number of degrees awarded increased by about 3 percent. Almost all of the growth came in the for-profit sector. At the same time, the for-profit share of the overall market remains miniscule. Four-year for-profit institutions number 453; 844 two-year for-profit institutions exist, and there are 1,382 less than two-year for-profits. Of the almost 2.3 million degrees awarded at four-year institutions, for-profits only account for 160,000. Similarly, of the over half-million two-year degrees, for-profits account for barely over 10 percent.

Private not-for-profit and for-profit four-year institutions offered similar costs for their degrees—on average, about $17,000 at private nonprofits and 14,000 at for-profits. The significant discrepancy in cost is evident in the much lower average cost at the public institution for in-state tuition—about $5,500. Similarly, the average price for tuition at public two-year institutions is about $2,205, whereas at for-profit two-year institutions the cost rises to $11,924 (National Center for Education Statistics [NCES], 2007). Again, such a point is important because the public institution is able to offer in-state tuition at a reduced price because the citizenry supports these institutions through tax dollars. This subsidy is based on the assumption that the institution is a public good available to all qualified citizens; without this public good, the citizenry would be less well off.

As noted, a concern about for-profit colleges and universities has to do with the quality of their offerings. Unlike traditional institutions, at which accreditation is the norm, for-profit colleges and universities (FPCUs) frequently lack regional or state accreditation. Although the growth of the absolute number of institutions has risen, as has the number of degrees that have been awarded, the retention and completion rates at FPCUs are closely guarded secrets by the boards that run them. The National Consumer Law

Center (2005), for example, has commented "numerous companies have been the subject of private lawsuits and government investigations alleging market abuses and other serious violations. Misrepresentations frequently involve inflated claims that students will graduate and find jobs" (p. 1). The problem revolves around the ability to capture completion rate and placement information from the FPCUs. Federal data provides completion rates for for-profits, but not retention or attrition rates. A great many negative reports have alleged that FPCUs either inflated their numbers or simply falsified data because of a weak or non-existent regulatory environment. To be sure, negative reports also abound in the public and private nonprofit sectors; the difference is a matter of degree. Although for-profits account for a meager percentage of overall institutions and degrees, they have a much greater percentage of negative reports about quality, completion, and employment of their graduates.

Accordingly, one way to summarize the FPCU environment is to recognize that they are the fastest-growing institutional type in postsecondary education, but they still account for only a miniscule share of the market. And yet they have attracted a great deal of attention with regard to product oversight and quality. On the one hand, critics have alleged that regulatory oversight is weak, and on the other, they have argued that the quality of the product is weak. All of these points are important as regards a discussion of the public good. If these institutions warrant public support, their growth should be welcomed. At the same time, the public good is not an unexamined product irrespective of quality or effectiveness. If public monies are put forward for a public good regardless of the form that receives those public monies, then of necessity there will be increased regulatory oversight.

Examining the Public Good

Traditionally, public goods have been characterized by three key terms: non-rivalry, non-excludability, and externalities (Vaknin, 2003). The idea of *non-rivalry* is that extending the service or providing the good to an additional individual or group is insignificant. As opposed to a private good, which is enjoyed only by those who own it, a public good is available to anyone who partakes of it. A personal car is a private good; the owner decides who rides in the car and where it goes; in part, the subway is a public good because it is subsidized. Everyone is able to ride on the subway; even though a passenger must pay a price, the cost is subsidized. *Non-excludability* means what it suggests: no one can be excluded from a public good, or from participating in the cost. The citizenry pays for the construction of the subway; no one is barred from traveling on it. Individuals also do not have the option to opt out of the cost for the creation and maintenance of the public good. Public goods, states Sam Vaknin (2003), "impose costs and benefits on others—individuals or firms—outside the marketplace and their effects are only partially reflected in prices and market transactions" (p. 1). Such a comment underscores the idea of *externalities:* public goods defy market classification, because they are worth more than they cost (although their actual cost often cannot be determined).

The classic example of a public good is a lighthouse. Society benefits from the lighthouse—a ship steers clear of the rocky shore and brings needed materials to port. Public monies may well support the salary of a lighthouse watchperson, but the money goes toward a larger good than simply remuneration for the individual who is employed. National defense is another public good. When individuals are born, their addition to the country does not increase the cost of the public good of defense. All individuals bear the cost of the defense through taxes. The good is also something that is usually underproduced in the market because not enough profit can be generated to make the good viable.

The decision about whether something is a public good also shifts over time. In the nineteenth century, protection from a fire was the responsibility of private companies that individuals paid to protect their homes. If a fire started in someone's house, then the private company arrived to put out the fire. If the fire spread to a neighbor's, but the neighbor did not have fire insurance from that specific company, then the private company let the house burn. Eventually, such a strategy seemed ill-advised, and fire protection became a public good. Fire companies supported through public monies existed in local communities and raced to put out fires irrespective of whose house had caught fire.

Conversely, police are a public good that is becoming privatized. A generation ago, security in a city meant that the police patrolled the streets as a public good. Over the last generation, however, the upper class in urban centers has felt unsafe, and the result is the rise of private security firms and gated communities.

Similarly, farm subsidies were once thought of as a public good. Farm subsidies in the United States date to the Great Depression of the 1930s. In

1932, the farm population was 25 percent of the nation's total. President Franklin D. Roosevelt signed the Agricultural Adjustment Act (AAA) in 1933 because conditions on farms were dire—not simply for individuals, but for the nation. In 1932, farm income was a third of what it had been in 1929. Agricultural prices were less than half of what they have been before the Depression took hold. Fear, anger, and rebellion gripped the countryside because of farm foreclosures. The Roosevelt administration's assumption was that the country needed farm supports to grow out of the depression, and that such subsidies aided not just those who directly received the public monies, but everyone. Fifty years later, however, farm subsidies are little more than political patronage for those who live in farm states. The family farm is a vestige of the last century. Subsidies today support large companies that in turn support candidates for office. Surely if farm subsidies are eliminated, the country will not face the crises it had in the early 1930s. The country is far removed from the kind of nation we were in 1929. My point here is less an exegesis on farm subsidies and more to highlight how the definition of the public good changes over time due to the conditions in which it exists.

Higher Education as a Public Good

Higher education is no different from other public goods. Mass public higher education did not occur until the late nineteenth century with the passage of the Morrill Acts in 1862 and 1890 (Nevins, 1962). The underlying assumption was that the country benefited if more of its citizenry attended a college or university, and the form for that to occur was a public institution. The content of postsecondary education was primarily aimed at training in the agricultural and mechanical sciences, although the precise nature of the curriculum was left in the hands of the faculty. The remainder of the nineteenth century and the early part of the twentieth century saw a discussion about the definition of the public good of higher education to really be an extension of that which occurred in K–12 education. If parents could afford to send their offspring to a private institution such as Stanford or Harvard Universities, then by all means they should, but public monies were reserved for public institutions.

The idea of higher education as a public good also followed along traditional lines, albeit with "real-world" interpretations. The idea of nonrivalry, of course, is an ideal type that breaks down even with examples such as national defense or purified drinking water. Presumably, the cost of defending citizens in Guam from attack differs from the cost of defending a Kansan. To lay pipelines for purified drinking water is different for a rural citizen in Montana than for an urban one in New York. An influx of students into public higher education raises the costs of the public good in a way that an increase in the citizenry does not for national defense. Nevertheless, a state system that has institutions such as a public community college, a public state college or university, and a public research university ensures that the citizenry will have access to a public good and not be excluded in large part because of the expense of a postsecondary education. Just as the state subsidizes the subway for its riders, so, too, does it subsidize public postsecondary institutions for its students.

The argument over public higher education as a public good has largely turned on two issues: form and definition. As with their confreres in K–12 education, individuals have asked why public monies go to an institution rather than a person. Why not let the consumers choose how to spend his or her money rather than force them to choose public institutions? The call for expanded choices for the consumer has less to do with the quality of the content—curricular offerings—and more to do with the manner in which learning gets conveyed. Public institutions, in general, have set geographic boundaries, and courses are offered at specific times. Some will point out that those times are arranged for the convenience of the faculty rather than the convenience of the consumer. The assumption here is that enabling the citizenry to receive a postsecondary degree is still in the public good and hence deserving of public monies; what is questionable is the organizational form that provides the education.

For-profit providers have built their course offerings in a way that any savvy business person would build a business—the courses are offered at convenient times and locations. Rather than the lock-step fifteen-week semester that begins around Labor Day, takes a break over the Christmas holidays, and starts again in January only to end for the summer interregnum in May, for-profits are more likely to offer classes around the year and not be wedded to any particular calendar. Classes might be offered in the evening or on weekends to suit the needs of working people, and a class is as likely to be held in a vacant room in a shopping mall as it is on a "campus." Thus, just as the K–12 discussion has morphed from a small constituency—Catholics—desirous of a specific kind of institution for their children to a larger discussion of school choice, so, too, in higher education has the discussion moved toward wondering why public monies support institutions rather than people.

Such an argument is possible because the definition of higher education has been framed in a manner akin to K–12 education. The role of public schools is to educate children; the role of public higher education is to educate adolescents and adults. If the definition of public and for-profit institutions is equivalent, then naturally the criticisms of one become conjoined with the other. Further, for-profit colleges and universities also are able to point to a diverse constituency with regard to race, class, and gender. That is, some might argue that public higher education increases access to a postsecondary education for previously disenfranchised groups. However, the percentage of African American students at for-profits, for example, is almost twice as large as at public institutions, and a larger percentage of Hispanics make up the total population of for-profits than TCUs (NCES, 2007). One can reasonably conclude that no claim can be made that public postsecondary education is doing a demonstrably better job at increasing access to higher education than are FPCUs.

The responses by those who reject the idea of public funding of for-profits generally has focused on content: public higher education's curriculum has a more noble purpose than merely training, hence, FPCUs should be looked on as suspect and certainly not deserving of public monies. To be sure, certain classes in some TCUs have had the purpose of helping students think through thorny problems and by doing so have made them more publicly engaged—even though the measurement of such engagement has proven to be difficult. The argument falls down, however, when we look at the vast panoply of institutions and courses offered under the aegis of the public good. Surely, an auto mechanics course at a community college or an accounting course at a state college have the potential of doing little more than training students for employment. The point is not that these courses fall short of expectations, but that not every course in every public institutions is, or should be, geared toward liberal learning.

Supporters of FPCUs will add that providing gainful employment for individuals ought to be seen as enabling individuals to participate in a democracy, although such courses differ from the more vigorous kinds of argumentation one might see in some classes on some campuses. The result is that the criticism that for-profits do not provide the citizenship function of liberal learning might be acknowledged, but one also must accept that the vast majority of public institutions do not do that either.

However, public higher education has never been about only schooling and learning. A public good is not intended to benefit only those make use of it. Fire stations exist to protect everyone. The national defense protects all citizens. Farm subsidies during the Depression were intended to help not only the farmers who received the public largesse, but also the country. Thus, the private benefits of a postsecondary education—if it is a public good—needs to help more than the individuals who receive that public education, and in large part, that is why public institutions have been accorded the right to offer that service. The expectation has been that in return for public support, colleges and universities will benefit all of the citizenry, even if indirectly, irrespective of whether individuals actually attend the institution or not. If public universities are simply oriented to serving the private interests of individuals—of increasing the wealth of its graduates—then why ought not public monies be spread about all types of institutions who are able to do that in different forms and with different contents?

Stuart Tannock (2006) has a response that is worth quoting at length:

> Universities serve the public good, all else being equal, not when they contribute to "economic development" in some abstract and general sense, but when they help to increase the wealth and well-being of all individuals together; and more specifically, when they work to ensure that the college-educated do not gain at the expense of the non-college educated. (p. 45)

Tannock's comment, while provocative, also points to the possibility that higher education should be privatized. On the one hand, Tannock usefully argues that the purpose of postsecondary institutions has to be more than merely as educational training centers for those who attend them. On the other hand, Tannock's suggestion brings into question not merely the form that provides the public good—public colleges and universities—but also whether such a good is even worthy of public monies. In effect, Tannock makes the helpful point that universities are primarily oriented to serving the private interests of individuals and if they are, then why have they any right to public funding more than other organizations that serve private interests? Such an observation, if followed to its logical conclusion, moves not merely toward defunding the form of the public good—public institutions—but also the definition itself—higher education.

Tannock is critical of what he calls "window dressing" (p. 47) by institutions when an institution's leaders adopt activities such as service learning, community outreach, or student volunteerism under the guise that institutions desire to be involved in the community, but in practice they are not. Again, such a comment is particularly important when looking at the vast panoply of public postsecondary institutions. How many public institutions might be honestly focused on significant efforts at community engagement, if Tannock's call were heeded?

Indeed, Tannock goes so far as to suggest that

> [i]f universities are unable—or worse, unwilling—to tackle such issues as the wage gap, then perhaps a compelling public-good argument can be made that the non-college educated in this country . . . would be better off spending their tax dollars on themselves directly, rather than allowing them to be siphoned through an increasingly expensive, elitist, unresponsive, and un-civic system of higher education. (p. 48)

In one sense, the suggestion nicely fits with the FPCU argument, although I am certain Tannock has no such desire to support for-profit education as a method to supplant public higher education insofar as the tax dollars citizens are saved ultimately benefit the wealthy, and undoubtedly compromise the ability of the poor to afford any kind of postsecondary education. Tuition at public institutions is kept relatively low through public subsidies, and tuition at private nonprofit and for-profit institutions is paid for by the poor through publicly supported financial aid.

Tannock and others actually believe that the idea of education and the market is anathema, and that rather than ape market tendencies, public higher education has to be more focused on educational purpose. John McMurtry (1991), for example, has argued, "The overriding goal of corporate agents in the marketplace is to maximize private money profits. The overriding goal of educational agents in schools, college, and universities is to advance and disseminate shared knowledge" (p. 211). Such an opposition assumes that knowledge is to be shared openly rather than consumed privately. The motivations of those in the market are to increase the worth of the goods, whereas knowledge accumulation is the growth of cognitive capacity, which is frequently in direct opposition to capital development. The result is that those in education ought not pursue the market model but instead return to a devotion of civic engagement.

Those who argue for postsecondary institutions as a public good have never denied that an educational degree has private benefits for an individual. As Lazerson (1998) has noted:

> Higher education came to simultaneously embody both a public good— beneficial to the nation's economy, protective of its national defense, opening up new avenues of knowledge, and able to realize equality of educational opportunity—and a private benefit so that everyone who possessed it substantially improved their access to higher income, status and security. (p. 65)

The point, then, is not that someone accrues personal benefit through a public good, but that the personal benefit cannot be the only, or even the primary, benefit. From this perspective, a public good has to entail more than the traditional components I outlined of nonrivalry, non-excludability, and externalities. Perhaps commonsensical, but nevertheless, a public good also has to demonstrate a good for the public. Such a claim assumes that the form of the public good is quite important—a public institution will undertake actions that a private company is likely not to do because of the profit motive.

Although contexts certainly change, one wonders if those who call for higher education to "reclaim" a sense of civic purpose are nostalgic for a day that may never have existed, or that is impossible to create today. Patricia Gumport (2000), for example, states, "I am concerned that technical, market imperatives run wild, urging colleges and universities to adapt to short term market demands, to redeploy resources, in an effort to reposition themselves with an increasingly competitive context" (p. 70). Such sentiments may precisely describe how certain institutions respond to increased pressures from the marketplace, but the comment also assumes that the social compact was much more formulated in the past than it is today. Similarly, Adrianna Kezar (2004) writes that the social charter of higher education "can be aligned with a communitarian philosophy in which the community takes precedence over the individual. . . . For much of the last hundred years, higher education in the United States can be seen as mirroring the communitarian belief system with its emphasis on such goals as developing leaders, serving the needs of regional and local communities, or acting as a social critic" (p. 435). While one may agree with such sentiments, I am unclear why we think that today's postsecondary institutions are not developing leaders, serving regional or local needs, and acting as a social critic in at least as great a proportion to yesterday's institutions? I have seen no evidence confirming that today's postsecondary institutions are less adept at fulfilling the public good—or, more important, I have seen no evidence that says yesterday's institutions did a better job.

To be sure, land grant institutions came about to develop the public good. In large part, however, their purpose was aimed at "content"—training in the mechanical and agricultural sciences. Such a purpose was critical in the nineteenth century, because no one else offered such training on a widespread basis. Today, however, multiple providers are able to offer such classes. Some land grants also offered agricultural extension services to local farmers, but such a service is less in need today than it was in the early twentieth century.

Some who long for the public good of the past also will look to the sweeping statements of college presidents such as Daniel Coit Gilman of Johns Hopkins University, William Rainey Harper of the University of Chicago, or Charles Eliot of Harvard University about the obligation of academe to society, but what is one to make of such statements? In Gilman's inspirational inaugural address, he said that universities should "make for less misery among the poor, less ignorance in the schools, less fraud in business, less folly in politics" (Benson, Harkevy, & Hartley, 2005, p. 193). Noble sentiments, to be sure.

Parenthetically, of course, these men led private universities, but we could easily find similar presidential statements today at the same institutions. Thus, I find no evidence for the assertion that "the democratic mission served as *the* central mission for the development of the American research university" (Benson, Harkevy, & Hartley, 2005, p. 193). Indeed, one might look to these same institutions at the time that their presidents made such comments and merely examine their exclusion of the poor, women, students of color, and gays and lesbians from the halls of learning and question how well they served the democratic mission of which they spoke. Such sentiments are admirable goals to aspire to, but we ought not to romanticize the past.

The exception, of course, also does not prove the rule. Because a public university such as the University of California at Berkeley's having created a misguided relationship with a pharmaceutical company such as Novartis or the energy giant BP is certainly a cause for concern, we cannot then simply conclude that a systemic rupture has taken place between what was and what is. My concern is that more often than not, such examples of postsecondary institutions that have lost their way (although helpful) shed light on present concerns but do nothing to demonstrate how institutions functioned in the past. Surely numerous examples exist of public postsecondary institutions that never fulfilled the romantic notion of the public good that many authors desire.

The Way Forward

Brian Pusser points out that if higher education is to be thought of as a public good, then it needs to be conceived as a public sphere (2006, 2007). Following Habermas, Pusser (2007) thinks of the public sphere as

> A space beyond the control of either the State or private interests where public conversation, deliberation and innovation can take place. It is also a site of contest, where various perspectives on the State and on private interests can be freely and publicly debated, and where social identities may be forged. (p. 38)

Such a comment is certainly in keeping with one key function of postsecondary institutions that is commonly associated with the nonprofit and public sectors, but not at all in the for-profit sector. Academic freedom, free speech, and public discussions and debates about the great issues of the day, large and small, have been hallmarks of some institutions at some points in their histories. The free speech movement at the University of California, Berkeley is but one example in a long history of an institution's participants speaking out on an important topic. These events may be campus-wide undertakings such as protests of the Vietnam War in the 1960s or singular actions in a classroom by way of a faculty member provoking thoughtful discussion on thorny issues. Recently, for example, the president of Iran was invited to speak at Columbia University in the midst of protest over his visit to the United States.

I do not deny that many public institutions have made little use of their ability to be a public sphere or that many institutions have mishandled the manner in which such events have been handled. And yet, simply because some citizens do not make use of their right to free speech, or because others misuse theirs, does not mean we should eliminate free speech in the

United States. Such a point is useful and not necessarily in conflict with the goals of for-profit higher education or a view of postsecondary education in a marketplace in a capitalistic economy. As I have argued elsewhere (Tierney and Hentschke, 2007; Tierney, 2006), my purpose here is to lessen the perception between traditional and for-profit providers that there is a gulf between both entities and that any chance of accommodation with one another is impossible.

Rather, I see the need for both entities that have different, yet overlapping interests. As noted repeatedly in this chapter, certainly not all public postsecondary institutions serve the public good in a manner that is clamored for by those who see greater public and civic engagement. At the same time, as observed elsewhere in this book, the market for higher education is growing exponentially and taking forms that vary significantly from the traditional format that public institutions have employed over time. However, simply that the market for higher education experiences rapid growth, with for-profit providers as one plausible outlet, ought not to suggest that the public sphere of which Pusser (2007) writes should be eliminated. Essentially, I am asking: what might be done to maintain the traditional role of higher education as a public sphere that serves the public good, broadly defined, while the public also develops a more protean notion of how various providers might effectively serve certain aspects of a public good? Three responses are appropriate:

Reemphasize that public institutions need to be more engaged with their publics and recognize their import as democratic spheres. Such a point ought to be a part of any strategic conversation at an institution and in a state. My assumption is that the responses of some public institutions, especially community colleges, will not differ very greatly from the kind of responses that for-profit providers would claim—an educated citizenry is a public and private good. However, the expectation ought to be, and at some institutions there is vigorous discussion, about how they might foment debate about controversial local, state, and national issues. Further, additional institutions need to be involved in their communities in significant ways that move beyond Tannock's charge of window dressing and address the very real needs that local and regional communities face. And still others need to make a better case for how the institution's research serves a vital public interest.

Recognize that for one key aspect of higher education as a public good—that of education and training—the form of the provider is less important than the quality of the content. Such an observation is not in conflict with the immediate response above about the importance of a vibrant public sphere. However, at a time when the need for postsecondary education continues to grow such that multiple organizational forms need to be enabled, one can no longer reject out of hand that one provider should be excluded from education and training. Rather, it seems pertinent that unless one provider is better than another at educating individuals, preference should be provided to expand the forms of organization that offer postsecondary education.

Ensure that all providers face adequate regulation and oversight particularly with regard to completion rates, retention, attrition, financial aid payments, defaults, and job placement. Any company, of course, faces normal regulatory oversight to ensure compliance with good business practices and to protect the consumer against fraud. What I suggest here, however, goes beyond typical demands for good business from private companies.

I have made the argument that access to quality education, as defined by degree completion and job placement, is part of the public good of higher education, and that multiple providers should be able to lay claim to providing those services. However, those providers should expect to face increased regulation and oversight. The federal and state government has the capacity to monitor dropout rates, fiscal defaults, and job placement. My guess is that some public, private nonprofit, and (especially) for-profit sectors will resist such attempts. For-profits, in particular, are particularly hesitant to disclose such outcomes for fear of lessening the worth of their product. The point, however, is that their product is part of the public good. If an institution is unwilling or unable to provide transparent information related to issues such as retention and job placement, then it should be denied access to public monies.

My point here has been to argue that the definition of the "public good" in general, and with regard to higher education in particular, is a protean notion that changes over time and has multiple facets to it. What the country expected of postsecondary education in the late nineteenth century, when largely one class of people received a degree, is different from what we ought to expect in the kind of country we inhabit in the twenty-first century. Unlike a fire station or a lighthouse, which has largely one function—to prevent fires or to guide ships—higher education's purpose is multiple.

Further, the need for postsecondary education is growing, and one of those functions can be offered by more than one provider. However, for the maintenance, if not the furtherance of the public good, adequate protections need to be put in place to ensure that public monies are invested wisely. Such a recommendation is likely to bother those who have a purist sense of the public good and believe that only public institutions are able to provide public goods. For-profit providers are also likely to bemoan increased regulation and argue that a private business should not have to act like a public organization. Although such concerns are to be expected, if we are to meet the economic, social, and philosophical needs of the United States in the twenty-first century, some form of these recommendations need to be considered.

References

Benson, L., Harkavy, I., & Hartley, M. (2005). Integrating a commitment to the public good into the institutional fabric. In A. J. Kezar, T. C. Chambers, J. C. Burkhardt, & Associates (Eds.), *Higher education for the public good* (pp. 185–216). San Francisco: Jossey-Bass.

Gumport, P. (2000). Academic restructuring: Organizational change and institutional imperatives. *Higher Education, 39,* 67–91.

Kezar, A. (2004). Obtaining integrity? Reviewing and examining the charter between higher education and society. *The Review of Higher Education, 27*(4), 429–459.

Lazerson, M. (1998). The disappointments of success: Higher education after World War II. *Annals of the American Academy of Political and Social Science, 559,* 64–76.

McMurtry, J. (1991). Education and the market model. *Journal of Philosophy of Education, 25*(2), 209–217.

National Center for Education Statistics. (2007). *Postsecondary institutions in the United States: Fall 2006 and degrees and other awards conferred: 2005–06* (NCES Publication No. 2007-166). Washington, DC: Author.

National Consumer Law Center. (2005). *Making the numbers count: Why proprietary school performance data doesn't add up and what can be done about it.* Boston: Author.

Nevins, A. (1962). *The origins of the land-grant colleges and state universities: A brief account of the Morrill Act of 1862 and its results.* Washington, DC: Civil War Centennial Commission.

Pusser, B. (2006). Reconsidering higher education and the public good: The role of public spheres. In W. G. Tierney (Ed.), *Governance and the public good* (pp. 11–27). Albany, NY: SUNY Press.

Pusser, B. (2007). Higher education, markets, and the preservation of the public good. In D. W. Breneman, S. E. Turner, & B. Pusser (Eds.), *Earnings from learning: The rise of for-profit universities* (pp. 23–49). Albany, NY: SUNY Press.

Tannock, S. (2006, Spring). Higher education, inequality, and the public good. *Dissent, 53*(2), 45–51.

Tierney, W. G. (2006). *Trust and the public good: Examining the cultural conditions of academic work.* New York, NY: Peter Lang Publishers.

Tierney, W. G., & Hentschke, G. C. (2007). *New players, different game: Understanding the rise of for-profit colleges and universities.* Baltimore: The Johns Hopkins University Press.

Vaknin, S. (2003) *Is education a public good?* Retrieved August 29, 2004, from http://www.totse.com/en/politics/political_spew/iseducationapu173733.html.

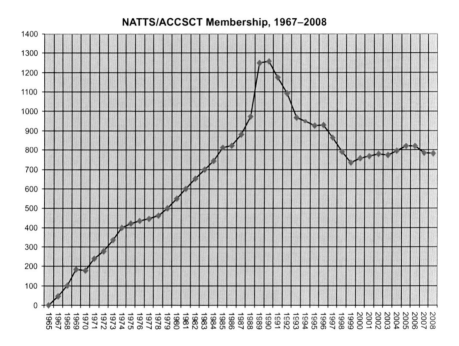

NATTS/ACCSCT Membership, 1967–2008

Complete List of Questions Posed at Accreditation Roundtable

* What are the major challenges facing accreditation in carrying out its mission of promoting and assuring quality in higher education?
* How can accreditation assure the government and the public that higher education institutions and programs are effective in achieving results, especially student learning outcomes?
* What is the relationship between accreditation and state accountability systems that measure and report performance outcomes for higher education and how can it be improved?
* What are the costs and benefits of accreditation for institutions and programs? How can accreditation help institutions and programs achieve greater improvements in performance and other benefits at lower costs?
* Do current accreditation standards and processes used by many accreditation organizations create barriers to innovation and diversity[,] including [to] new types of educational institutions and new approaches for providing educational services such as distance learning?
* How should regional accreditation respond to the growing national and global scale of education?
* Is there a need to improve the standardization and consistency of the standards and processes used by both regional and national accreditation organizations? How can accreditation help meet the increasing demand for public access to evidence of student outcomes and related information about institutions and program performance?

APPENDIX C

§602.16 Accreditation and Pre-accreditation Standards.

(a) The agency must demonstrate that it has standards for accreditation and, if offered, pre-accreditation that are sufficiently rigorous to ensure that the agency is a reliable authority regarding the quality of the education or training provided by the institutions or programs it accredits. The agency meets this requirement if –

  (1) The agency's accreditation standards effectively address the quality of the institution or program in the following areas:

    (i) Success with respect to student achievement in relation to the institution's mission, which may include different standards for different types of institutions or programs. Standards satisfying this criterion must include expected levels of performance that are either established by the agency, or established by the institution or program under subparagraphs (A) and (B). In addition –

(A) If the agency does not establish the expected levels of performance with respect to student achievement, the institution or program, at the institution or program level respectively, must –

  (1) Specify its goals for student achievement;

  (2) Establish the expected level of performance; and

  (3) Demonstrate its performance against those expected levels of performance using quantitative and qualitative evidence, including as appropriate external indicators.

(B) For pre-baccalaureate vocational programs and degree programs leading to initial professional licensure or certification, expected levels of performance must include completion rates, job placement rates, and, as applicable, pass rates on State licensing examinations or other appropriate measures of occupational competency.

(C) Every agency must demonstrate that its standards and processes allow it to evaluate whether the evidence provided by the institution or program shows that the institution's or program's performance is acceptable. In any instances when the institution or program establishes the expected levels of performance, the agency must also demonstrate that its standards and processes allow it to evaluate the institution's or program's expected levels of performance. The agency will take into account the institution's or program's use of other externally-set performance measures or criteria.

(D) Institutional accreditors will consider information provided by the institution about program level performance either in the aggregate, or at both the program level and in the aggregate, in making the institutional accreditation decision.

CONTRIBUTORS

Guilbert C. Hentschke is the Richard T. Cooper and Mary Catherine Cooper Chair in Public School Administration at the University of Southern California's Rossier School of Education.

Kevin Kinser is Associate Professor of Higher Education in the Department of Educational Administration and Policy Studies at State University of New York at Albany.

Vicente M. Lechuga is Assistant Professor of Higher Education Administration at Texas A&M University.

Michale S. McComis is Executive Director of the Accrediting Commission of Career Schools and Colleges (ACCSC).

Mark L. Pelish is Executive Vice President of Legislative and Regulatory Affairs for Corinthian Colleges, Inc.

Elise Scanlon is legal counsel with Drinker Biddle & Reath, LLP and served as the Executive Director of the Accrediting Commission of Career Schools and Colleges (ACCSC) from 1999–2009.

William G. Tierney is University Professor and Wilbur-Kieffer Professor of Higher Education, and Director of the Center for Higher Education Policy Analysis at the University of Southern California.

Also available from Stylus

The Impact of Culture on Organizational Decision Making
Theory and Practice in Higher Education
William G. Tierney

"Overall, this collection enables a fresh look at a set of theoretically rich articles, all of which have maintained their currency, on how we might think about and study postsecondary organizations. And while the chapters may not present any easy answers to those who work within higher education, the clear prose and cogent explanations certainly clarify how one's theory of organizational culture matters."—*Journal of College Student Retention*

The message of this book is that understanding organizational culture is critical for those who recognize that academe must change, but are unsure how to make that change happen.

Understanding College and University Organization
Theories for Effective Policy and Practice / Two Volume Set
James L. Bess, Jay R. Dee
Foreword by D. Bruce Johnstone

Volume I: The State of the System
Volume II: Dynamics of the System

A resource for leaders in higher education and a comprehensive textbook for graduate and master's courses.

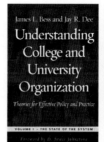 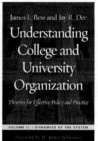

"Quite simply a tour de force. Not only have the authors written by far the broadest and deepest theoretical analysis of college and university organization I've seen, but they have clearly organized a complex topic, and written it engagingly. This will be seen as a landmark work in the field. It should be required reading for all who claim to understand higher education institutions and the behavior that goes on inside and around them."—*David W. Leslie, Chancellor Professor of Education, The College of William and Mary*

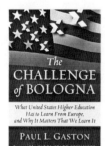

The Challenge of Bologna
What United States Higher Education Has to Learn from Europe, and Why It Matters that We Learn It
Paul L. Gaston
Foreword by Carol Geary Schneider

"American higher education is one of the great successes of the twentieth century. But like many others, I am concerned about losing our position of leadership. Paul Gaston is eminently qualified to respond to such concerns. He skillfully relates the Bologna priorities established in Europe a decade ago to current issues in American higher education—critically examining entrenched practices and calling for renewed emphasis on what is learned, rather than what is taught. Paul Gaston's analysis and proposal for a process of reform are clearly and compellingly presented. His work is worthwhile reading for anyone engaged in higher education."—*James E. Bundschuh, President, Marymount University, Virginia*

Sty/us 22883 Quicksilver Drive
Sterling, VA 20166-2102

Subscribe to our e-mail alerts: www.Styluspub.com